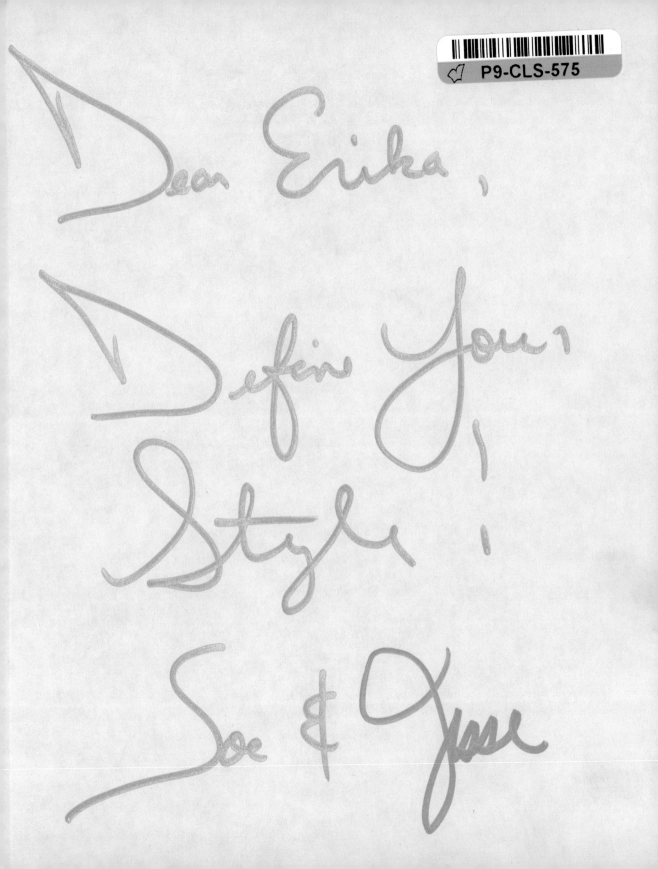

Dear Erika,

Define Your
Style!

Soe & Jesse

Nothing to Wear?

A 5-STEP CURE FOR
THE COMMON CLOSET

Nothing
to
Wear?

JESSE GARZA AND JOE LUPO

ILLUSTRATIONS BY RUBEN TOLEDO
ORIGINAL PHOTOGRAPHY BY PETER MURDOCK

HUDSON
STREET
PRESS

HUDSON STREET PRESS
Published by Penguin Group
Penguin Group (USA) Inc., 375 Hudson Street, New York, New York 10014, U.S.A.
Penguin Group (Canada), 90 Eglinton Avenue East, Suite 700, Toronto, Ontario,
    Canada M4P 2Y3 (a division of Pearson Penguin Canada Inc.)
Penguin Books Ltd, 80 Strand, London WC2R 0RL, England
Penguin Ireland, 25 St. Stephen's Green, Dublin 2, Ireland
    (a division of Penguin Books Ltd.)
Penguin Group (Australia), 250 Camberwell Road, Camberwell,
    Victoria 3124, Australia (a division of Pearson Australia Group Pty. Ltd.)
Penguin Books India Pvt. Ltd., 11 Community Centre, Panchsheel Park,
    New Delhi – 110 017, India
Penguin Books (NZ), cnr Airborne and Rosedale Roads, Albany,
    Auckland 1310, New Zealand (a division of Pearson New Zealand Ltd.)
Penguin Books (South Africa) (Pty.) Ltd., 24 Sturdee Avenue, Rosebank,
    Johannesburg 2196, South Africa

Penguin Books Ltd., Registered Offices: 80 Strand, London WC2R 0RL, England

First published by Hudson Street Press, a member of Penguin Group (USA) Inc.

First Printing, March 2006
10 9 8 7 6 5 4 3 2 1

Illustrations by Ruben Toledo
Original photography by Peter Murdock
Visual Therapy logo courtesy of Niche Studios.

H
HUDSON
STREET
PRESS   REGISTERED TRADEMARK—MARCA REGISTRADA

LIBRARY OF CONGRESS CATALOGING-IN-PUBLICATION DATA
Garza, Jesse.
Nothing to wear? : a 5-step cure for the common closet / Jesse Garza and Joe Lupo ; illustra-
    tions by Ruben Toledo ; original photograph by Peter Murdoch.
    p. cm.
ISBN 1-59463-028-3 (alk. paper)
1. Fashion—Psychological aspects.   2. Clothing and dress—Psychological aspects.   I. Lupo,
    Joe.   II. Title.
TT507.G368 2006
646'.34—dc22   2005025455

Printed in the United States of America
Set in Bembo with Futura and Amazone
Designed by Sabrina Bowers

To our clients:

our true inspiration

Acknowledgments

Neither Visual Therapy nor, subsequently, *Nothing to Wear?* would have been possible without our loving families, who have always nourished us, believed in us, and encouraged us to pursue our dreams. We especially thank Joan Weinstein, Jesse's mentor, whose voice is heard every day, and influences everything he does, and Stephen Gan, the first to acknowledge us as the "fashion SWAT team," which encouraged us to move forward to further develop our concept. We also thank our good friends at *The Oprah Winfrey Show* and *O* magazine for always thinking of us, as well as our friends at Bergdorf Goodman and Neiman Marcus.

Throughout our journey there have been many heroes who have

lifted us up, including Desiree Gruber and Hilla Narov and the team at Full Picture, who joined us early, supported our vision, and saw great possibilities for a big future. Julie Morgenstern, the light and inspiration, showed us that you can run your dream business and live to write about it. Joni Evans, our genius literary agent from William Morris, who made this book happen, and the motivation provided by Laureen Rowland, our publisher at Hudson Street Press, who kept us moving in the right direction. Special thanks are due to our incredible team past and present at Visual Therapy—Sarah Davidzuk, Kelly Hurliman, Georgia Mack, Michael Kramer, and Lani Rosenstock—whose efforts represent the backbone of our work, and to John McCarty for his excellent organizational skills.

Just as important as finding the right words was creating the right images to represent our ideas. For this, we thank our dear friends, Ruben and Isabel Toledo, for adding their magic touch to bring the book to life.

Contents

Foreword
How Visual Therapy Changed My Life!

I have a confession to make. I was never particularly interested in fashion. Sure, I appreciated nice fabrics such as cashmere, silks, and fine wool—and I always wanted to dress like a professional and look put together—but once I'd decided what I looked good in (in other words, once I'd established my "uniform"), that was the end of it. I didn't read fashion magazines. I hated to shop. I never judged people by what they wore, or by their sense of style.

As a professional organizer, my occupation is founded upon my ability to look past people's "stuff," and see the real person inside. Other people's focus on fashion seemed rather superficial to me.

Then I met up with Jesse Garza and Joe Lupo. And my attitude

changed. Through them, I discovered that what you wear can be a catalyst for the way you relate to the world, and how you care for and project yourself. Their "Visual Therapy" process is about so much more than fashion. It's about:

➤ discovering and expressing your fullest, most powerful self
➤ building a stronger, clearer communication with the world
➤ developing a more loving relationship with yourself

If this book attracted your attention, my guess is you are ready to make some big changes in your life. Your wardrobe, and having "nothing to wear," is only a part of what you'd like to change.

That was certainly true for me. Six months before working with Jesse and Joe, I'd begun a significant personal and professional transition. On a personal level, I was preparing myself for an empty nest. As a single mom, I had joyfully focused the lion's share of my time and energy on raising my daughter. It was a wonderful job, but with Jessi graduating high school and moving out in the fall, I was on the verge of a big identity shift.

Professionally, I was about to take my career to the next level with the publication of my first hardcover business book, *Making Work Work,* the result of four years of research and development. I was extremely proud of the material and felt ready to step out into the business platform and stay there, confident in my knowledge and expertise.

In anticipation of these changes, I felt ready to connect to the world in a new way—a more complete, more sustained way. Always one to attribute themes to years and phases of my life, I'd decided that this new stage of my life was about embracing my power. I began by changing the way I was eating, and created my own energy-based diet. By the time the summer came around, I'd lost a significant amount of weight. Not only did my clothes no longer fit, their styles seemed dated, boring, wrong.

I'd looked the same for the past fifteen years. I began experimenting (rather misguidedly) with different clothing styles, but I was stuck in a rut and without a clue. Enter Jesse Garza and Joe Lupo. Their mission: not to change me, just to kick up my look a notch.

I was excited and nervous on the day of our initial consultation. That Sunday afternoon, my doorbell rang, and upon opening the door, my heart just about leapt out of my chest. Standing there was an absolute dream team—two beautiful, well-put-together guys, radiating with the most open, genuine smiles and sparkling eyes.

I knew immediately that I had made the right choice. Before even looking in my closet, they sat me down in my living room and plied me with tons of questions. They wanted to know who I am, where I've been, and where I'm going. I instantly recognized that Jesse and Joe were working *from the inside out*; discovering who I was and dressing me for the life I wanted to live.

They asked me to name my favorite everything—color, place, flower, actress, etc. Answers didn't come easily to me, because I tend to pay more attention to others' needs and habits than to my own. They wanted to know who I admire in terms of look; I was embarrassed to admit that the only character that came to mind was Murphy Brown (though I look nothing like Candice Bergen) whose executive power and polish are very appealing. I also thought of the actress Demi Moore, for her natural beauty—but I was afraid to 'fess up to that one just yet.

They asked me to describe my current style. I had no words for it; I didn't speak the language of fashion. They prompted me: "Conservative?" Oh no, that sounded boring. "Chic?" I shrugged. "Sophisticated?" I had no idea! All I could say was that the most important thing to me was to be approachable, yet at the same time powerful.

A vocabulary began to take shape—suggesting my current style was conservative, the boys said they could see vestiges that indicated I used to be bohemian. So true! My background was in the theater, and I used to live in long, flowing skirts and dresses. How did they know?

Finally, they asked to look inside my closet and at the clothes I typically wear. I modeled my favorite, worn-to-death gray suit—the "business uniform" I always felt safest in. Their reaction: You're hiding in your clothes. It's too loose and boxy, we can't see you in there.

Okay, they had my attention. All of my suits were some version of this same cut. So, I pulled out my one little breakaway suit—a cuter, more modern, less traditional style. I put it on and modeled it with pride. Jesse and Joe were silent. Then, at the same time, they each announced, "It's the same suit!" It was hysterical. Here I thought this one was so different, but it was just another version of the same boxy look.

Observing that my clothes looked late eighties/early nineties, Jesse asked what was going on for me at that time. That's when I'd started my business, and when I'd made the switch from the bohemian look to business attire. I'd adopted a straight, neutral, elegant silhouette . . . sort of an Armani Man cut that I had believed projected strength and power in business.

Their vision was to put me in shorter jackets, with a more open neckline and tapered waist that would reveal my curves. Their proposal: You can have your power and still be feminine. A powerful business-*woman*, not just the powerful businessperson. It was a strange concept to me, but I was game. They were the experts, after all.

Wardrobe Clarification

I'd originally expected that I would box up and store the clothes that no longer fit (especially the more expensive items), but to my surprise, I found myself easily letting go simply by posing the three Visual Therapy questions about each garment: Do I love it? Is it flattering? Does it project the image I want to portray? Anything that didn't get a yes answer was given away or tossed.

Before I knew it, I had purged from my closet fourteen huge bags' worth of clothes. There were a few tough choices, including a sand-colored cashmere cardigan and green jacket that I loved, but finally I came around to getting rid of them because the colors weren't flattering. I was driven by the idea of creating room for new things and a new life.

With my closet now 80 percent empty, I suddenly experienced a deep moment of panic. Was I getting rid of too much? Had I gotten too slaphappy in tossing things? I felt empty, a bit lost, because little remained that was familiar to hold onto.

The boys assured me that although my closet was nearly empty now, soon it would be filled with things that would look and feel *amazing*. I reminded myself of my goal—to create a richer, more connected life—and reflected on the courage it takes to embrace change. I took a deep breath and relaxed into the fear. In under two hours, I was feeling better again.

That night, I slept like a baby. The emptiness in my closet promoted the feeling of sleeping by the ocean with a breeze moving through the room. I have come back to this image and drawn from it during other periods of growth and transition. Letting go creates space . . . and you need to trust that space. Because you are never alone—you have yourself, your spirit, your resources, all of which have gotten you where you are today. And you must trust that space you create will be filled with something extraordinary.

Filling in the Gaps

Next, the boys took me shopping to find clothes that would project the new me. They pulled things off the rack I never would have selected for myself—yet they all looked fabulous! I spent a good bit of

money on my new wardrobe, and felt a little anxious investing so much in it, but I had the sense that what I was <u>investing in was much more than clothing</u>, it was my new life.

Impact

And I was right. Noticing the impact my new look was having during the following few months was like being on an amusement park ride. Though not tall and tan, I felt a bit like the Girl from Ipanema, because everywhere I went, everyone seemed to say "ahhhh."

I seemed to project a whole new presence. Although I could always hold my own on stage and in business meetings, I now sensed the added power of my new look. Before, the neutrality of my clothes made me almost blend into a room. Yet, as soon as I began talking to people and connecting with them, they would see how smart, warm, and energetic I was.

With my new wardrobe, I commanded attention before I even uttered a word! In business meetings and onstage, a radiant power was projected simply by my appearance. It was an extraordinary feeling.

My new, polished look made me much more approachable, as well. Strangers everywhere began smiling at me and saying hello—at airports, on the street, in lobbies. Clients, staff, and even friends relaxed and opened up to me much more quickly than before. It was as though I had fully emerged. I now appeared much more present, open, and complete.

One Year Later . . .

The boys had told me they would want to see where I would be in a year's time—implying that after the makeover I was poised for great things and big changes . . . and were they ever right.

My relationships with friends, colleagues, and clients have grown richer and deeper. Following the fashion makeover, I embarked on a business makeover, with a similar goal: not to change the business, but build upon its fundamental strengths and take it to the next level. The result: Within six months my business expanded and grew dramatically. In addition, a long-envisioned corporate training division was launched to help companies increase employee productivity and job satisfaction.

I moved into the city, my social life is flourishing, and I feel like I am beginning a new chapter of my life.

But perhaps the most meaningful change is how great I feel and how easy it has been to sustain these changes—because they really were from the inside out. Even at home, by myself, I feel comfortable and pampered by my clothes. Wearing clothes that nurture and embrace me is a way to love and care for my body. My weight has stayed down because even on those occasions where I feel stressed, I no longer turn to food for comfort. My comfort is in my new body, my integral image, my power, which Jesse and Joe saw in me and brought out in a way I could never have done on my own.

My goal was to connect with the world in a new way, and the clothing makeover has played a huge part in my ability to achieve that goal. Jesse and Joe did for me with my clothing what I do for people as a professional organizer: They aligned who I am, what I want, and where I'm going with my wardrobe, and opened my eyes in ways that I never could've dreamed. The beauty of their approach is how authentic and organic it is: They impose nothing on you—they are here to help *you* become your best self.

Through them, I've learned that fashion, if in alignment with one's inner self, is among the most powerful statements you can make.

And now, as you embark on a similar journey, take a deep breath, get ready to discover your truest self, and have fun. Here's to the life you dream of and to becoming the greatest *you* that you can be!

Julie Morgenstern
New York Times best-selling author of *Organizing from the Inside Out*, and *Making Work Work*

Nothing to Wear?

It's Not Just About the Closet

Know first who you are, and then adorn yourself accordingly. —EPICTETUS

*W*hether dressing for a date, for work, or to take your kids to the park, chances are, you go through the same routine every day: You throw open your closet, stare blankly into the abyss, and mutter, *"I've got nothing to wear!"*

Millions of women just like you waste their time going through the same frustrating exercise *daily*. However different their lives may be—single or married, artist or accountant, six kids or no kids—their stories are similar. However much or little they spend on clothes and accessories, however much time they spend rifling through their closets, they can't understand why they always end up wearing the same four things, despite the fact that their closets are bursting with clothes.

Maybe you're reading this book because you simply want to look and feel a little bit better or different. Perhaps, at one time in your life, you were totally satisfied with your look, and you really enjoyed the art of getting dressed. Maybe you still like your look and only want to update it or turn it up a notch. But where to start?

One thing's for sure. You've no time to think about anything, much less about what to wear. You've lost interest, or perspective, or something—you're not sure what. All you know is that you go through the same pointless exercise every day, and something's got to change.

Visual Therapy to the rescue!

Style Is Found Only by Looking Inside Yourself

Each of us possesses an identity and an image. Our identity is who we are—our soul, our spirit, our personality. Our image is what we project—ourselves as others see us. One of the reasons you can feel lost or impatient in attempting to create your look is that you've lost touch with who you want the world to see.

To ensure great style, there must be a connectedness between identity and image—a clear alignment between the two. Very often there is a mismatch, or disconnect, between these elements that can lead to fashion frustration.

Projecting an image of ourselves that doesn't express who we are is always confusing, difficult, and exhausting. It can make us feel as if we're putting on a costume or assuming a role, forcing us to act like someone we are not.

As wardrobe consultants, we're trained to identify the clash or disparity between the way someone wishes to be perceived by others and how she actually looks (the self she sees in the mirror every day). To us, the signs of this disconnect are obvious. It's clearly evident in what someone chooses to wear, but to the wearer these hints may go unnoticed because she is simply too close to the problem to be objective. It's the old cliché: She "can't see the forest for the trees."

The goal of this book is to help you see this disconnect in your own look as clearly as we do, and then to walk you through the unique five-step process we've been successfully using with clients for more than ten years—to get you into the clothes that will have you looking and feeling like a million bucks.

Why the Disconnect?

The disconnect between your image and identity can be narrow or wide, and the solution can be as simple as infusing your existing wardrobe with some colorful, up-to-date accessories, or as thorough as weeding through and eliminating the old, the out-of-date, the too-tight, the too-loose in order to reestablish and realign your identity with your image. Five common situations that can lead to this type of disconnect:

1. Entering college
2. Entering or reentering the workforce, or getting a significant job or promotion
3. Marriage or divorce
4. Having children
5. A milestone birthday

No matter the extent of the disconnect, it can have powerful emotional and financial consequences. Identifying a disconnect can send you to extremes—over-shopping or overanalyzing what's new/newer/

newest to the point where you become a fashion victim, having lost any sense of the authentic style you once had. Or, it can send you into a fashion funk where you actually resist the idea of a style or wardrobe change, resign yourself to your current fashion plight, and simply give up. (This latter scenario tends to happen as you grow older. Barbara, an attractive woman in her fifties who felt uninspired by what she owned, believed she was "too old" to consider wearing the newest styles. As a result, she resigned herself to the way she always dressed, which, while extremely safe, left her looking and feeling dowdy.)

Similarly, when women become pregnant, or after they have become first-time mothers, their priorities shift, and their children become their focus. The little time they have to spend on themselves tends to push away thoughts of style and fashion. And yet, over time, they realize that by settling for what's easy, quick, and comfortable to wear—and childproof—they've lost touch with who they were and how they looked before they became someone's mom.

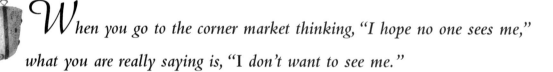

When you go to the corner market thinking, "I hope no one sees me," what you are really saying is, "I don't want to see me."

Our technique, Visual Therapy, teaches women that achieving a state of connectedness between your image and your identity is not about trying to mold yourself into someone you're not. It's about identifying and embracing who you are now. (This also means being realistic about what you have to work with physically, financially, logistically.) How to align your wardrobe choices with your life and your "fashion personality" so that you can best express yourself is the theme of this book. Visual Therapy offers you a systematic approach to making the right fashion choices *for you*.

What Is Visual Therapy?

Visual Therapy was created over a decade ago as a personal shopping service for women who don't have the time or don't know *how* to develop an individual look or unique fashion personality. Working with many women through the years, we began to see patterns in the way they shopped for clothes, how they approached the matter of style, and how they viewed themselves in relation to their wardrobe and fashion at different points in their lives.

What we discovered from observing these shopping patterns and approaches was that, for the most part, women look for a simple method to focus on their priorities, and to know that they can feel good about themselves and move through their world with confidence. Many of our clients claimed that they were unsure of their fashion choices and, as a result, often purchased things that were totally inappropriate for them. The feelings they had about their bodies and how they wanted to feel in their clothes (and, in effect, in their own skin) often were at odds with the choices they made. Some preferred to wear the same things year in and year out—or, many times a week—rather than to venture beyond their comfort zone and find a look that was right for them, particularly if they weren't sure what that look *was*.

Typically, our clients did everything they could to avoid facing reality. They didn't shop for clothes at all, or they shopped for the person they used to be or the woman they imagined themselves to be: thinner, heavier, older, younger, cooler, hipper. (You get the idea.) By not facing who they really were in their lives, it was nearly impossible for them to project the best, up-to-date version of themselves.

Having identified the symptoms, and made a diagnosis, we set out to create a prescription, ultimately called "Visual Therapy," that would cure this fashion malady and the closet chaos that accompanied it. And, after more than ten years honing our craft, we can safely say: *Projecting a comfortable, confident, and authentic style is about asking yourself the right lifestyle questions, and using your answers to create and amplify the best possible you.*

Visual Therapy is a prescription that works.

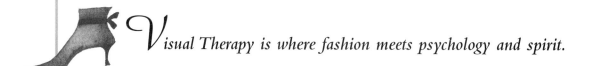

isual Therapy is where fashion meets psychology and spirit.

Fashion Should Be Fun, Not Frustrating

By following our prescription as directed, our clients are able to achieve something they've never had before: a sense of clarity about themselves and their personal style. This clarity provides them with the much needed direction to make the fashion choices that are right for *them*, and how to shop for clothes and accessories in ways that are smarter, less expensive, and more efficient.

Visual Therapy has not only brought about dramatic improvements in how our clients look but, more important, *how they feel about themselves.* Countless clients have commented that our five-step process has empowered them to revitalize their lives, knowing they are now making the most of what they have, looking their best (to themselves and to others), and feeling more confident, connected, and in control.

How to Use This Book

Consider these pages your very own Visual Therapy style consultant, in lieu of having Jesse and Joe live, on location, in the flesh, one-on-one. In fact, it's still one-on-one, but rather than face-to-face, it's more of an over-the-shoulder whisper in your ear.

In this book, we'll walk you through our five-step cure for the common closet. It will leave you feeling confident, calm, and clearly well dressed. Here's how:

Step #1: Define Your Style

Defining your style gives you a place to begin. It's a way to uncover and come to grips with who you are, to determine what is appropriate and inappropriate to your personal style (and why), and to identify which exciting fashion directions or possibilities exist for you.

Step #2: Edit Your Wardrobe

Here you will learn how to take a hard look at all the clothes crammed together in your closet and begin to understand why, despite the magnitude of stuff you own, you can never find anything to wear. This step makes it easy—and fun—to let go, move forward, and set yourself free. It teaches you how to perform a thorough love-it-or-leave-it examination of your entire wardrobe, leaving you—and your shelf space—open to new possibilities.

Step #3: Fill in the Gaps

Here's where you get to shop—yes, shop!—for the missing pieces, items like jackets, pants, and tops to add to your edited wardrobe to give you a variety of looks for different occasions. It's shopping, but shopping with a purpose and a clear image in mind.

Step #4: Pull It All Together

Now we'll show you how to create a variety of optimal looks. You'll learn to access them quickly and easily, so that getting dressed for any purpose at any time (yes, even in the morning) will be stress free, and perhaps even something to look forward to.

Step #5: Nurture the New You

Once you've made Visual Therapy a permanent part of your daily activity—an ongoing, self-educating process for keeping your new-found sense of style focused and moving in the right direction, that is, forward—you'll continue to be renewed with fresh ideas for exciting new looks.

Each step in the Visual Therapy process builds on the preceding one. Like bricks in a wall, they form a logical, systematic, and orderly way to establish a firm foundation. We prescribe this formula to our clients to help them develop or improve upon their sense of style, then to optimize that style, in a way that is integrated with their own personality and goals. To achieve the same results with this book as we do our clients—results that will save you from reinventing the wheel each time you dress—we suggest that you take our Visual Therapy prescription "as directed."

As a preview, take a look at a "before and after" client story, whose outlook on life was genuinely changed by the Visual Therapy process:

Symptom: Teri (her name has been changed, as are all the others in this book) is an attractive, sexy woman in her late thirties. Living in the year-round warm climate of Southern California, she had always projected a youthful, California beach-girl look. Then Teri had her first child, after which she retained much of her pregnancy weight. This meant that most of her size 6 pre-pregnancy clothes didn't fit anymore. This alone was depressing enough, but with a new baby to care for, getting too little sleep, and adjusting to the major lifestyle change of motherhood, shopping for herself wasn't even a consideration.

Enter the sweat suits, the oversized shirts and her husband's T-shirts, the uniform she donned day after day. On a good day, when she had a *little* time to herself, the most she could manage was a shower, a ponytail, and maybe some lip gloss which, instead of making her feel better, somehow only made her feel worse. For the first time in her life, Teri was overweight and felt exhausted. She stopped caring about what she looked like and became disillusioned, depressed, and defeated. Her "style" (she would laugh at the mere mention of that word) certainly reflected these feelings.

Prescription: By going through the five steps of Visual Therapy, Teri saw new possibilities. She learned that she could still be as attractive and sexy in a size 10 as she had been in a size 6—if she would just accept the changes in her body and in her life. She was no longer in her twenties, but a new mom and heading toward forty. By learning to accept these changes, she could let go of her former self and began to

Teri

Bohemian-Chic

R.T.

feel okay about celebrating who she is now. She learned to embrace and project a more grown-up image, a more sophisticated version of herself, while maintaining her youthful joie de vivre.

Outcome: Through Visual Therapy, Teri learned how to take what was still useable of her old wardrobe and add to it at minimal cost to achieve an authentic, fresh new look. When did she find the time, you might ask? In committing to doing Visual Therapy, she dedicated a certain amount of time for herself, and found that her mother, who lived nearby, was thrilled to be asked to babysit her first grandchild.

What was the impact of her transformation on herself and others?

Teri felt alive again. She felt sexier and more attractive but, most of all, she felt *in control.* She was more carefree and fun to be around, and could focus on the joy and wonder of motherhood. By revealing and removing the disconnect between the image she projected and who she was inside, and then addressing that issue head-on, Teri was able to come to terms with and love who she is today, and to flourish as that person.

It's Easier Than You Think

Not sure whether Visual Therapy is for you? Here's a list of a few other "symptoms" and "prescriptions." We'll bet you see yourself in one (or more) of them.

Symptom: "Visual Therapy won't work for me because I don't have time to fuss with my appearance."

Prescription: What you are really saying is, "You don't have time for yourself." You owe it to yourself to *make* the time. It benefits your physical, mental, and spiritual well-being. Visual Therapy's proactive approach to shaping your wardrobe so that it works for you, and organizing your closet so you have fast, easy access to that wardrobe, will enable you to carve out the time. It shows you how to go about looking your best with a foolproof techniques for making the job seem effortless. And the benefits really do spill over into how you feel about the rest of your life.

Symptom: *"Visual Therapy won't work for me because I'm a stay-at-home mom; I don't need to get all dressed up."*

Prescription: Looking good isn't the same as dressing up. If you are a stay-at-home mom, it is even *more important* for you to look your best so that you will feel comfortable in your own skin. The more dissatisfied you become with that glimpse of yourself you catch in the mirror, the more dissatisfied you become with the inner you. This can lead to a downward spiral and a dependence on doughnuts, sweatpants, and soap operas! By looking your best, you will feel better about yourself, and about your place in the world. Visual Therapy is a way to give yourself needed feedback and make it an integral part of your day-to-day life.

Symptom: *"Visual Therapy won't work for me because I can't afford to buy a whole new wardrobe."*

Prescription: Visual Therapy is not necessarily about spending a huge sum of money on clothes all at once. First, you build a solid foundation by developing a list of clothing needs after you have edited your wardrobe. Then, you cross each item off your list as you can afford to purchase them. This enables you to build your wardrobe in stages without breaking the bank. The result will be a wardrobe and closet that are more compact and more manageable, consisting of no more—and no less—than what really works for you.

Symptom: *"Visual Therapy won't work for me because I'll have to keep up with all the latest trends."*

Prescription: Visual Therapy does not mean becoming a fashion victim. In fact, it is a process for establishing your fashion priorities so that you don't feel you have to spend every penny on the latest, greatest accessory instead of paying your utilities. It is a disciplined approach to updating, refining, or reinventing your style in a knowledgeable, money- and time-saving way.

Symptom: *"Why do I need Visual Therapy when I only need to look good at work?"*

Prescription: Of course you don't have to be dressed up twenty-four hours a day. But you need consistency in your closet in order to look good in each area of your life. That way, you will consistently feel positive about yourself, and project that message. For example, have you ever seen a photo of a celebrity who always looks fabulous on the red carpet but, caught in her off-hours, looks like a homeless person? Her life is "spinning out of control," the headline will scream. And we tend to believe it because the difference in image is so great. It's the same with you. Look great at work *and* in the other areas of your life and your headline will read: "She's in control and consistent, she's got it going on."

Symptom: *"Visual Therapy won't work for me until I lose some weight."*

Prescription: Wrong! Visual Therapy is about embracing your body as it is, not making an issue of it in order to hold yourself back. Defining your style puts you on the right path. If you want or need to shed pounds, do it for health reasons, and because it makes you feel good about yourself. The idea is to look and feel your best.

Visual Therapy will help you edit your wardrobe like a professional organizer, but in a way that will help you understand your fashion personality and match your style to it. It provides not merely a remedy but a cure, a *total solution*: a prescription to help you understand the look you want to project, and the tools necessary to achieve it.

So, what are you waiting for? Let's get started.

Visual Therapy Step #1:

Define Your Style

Only wear clothes that make you feel alive. —VALENTINO

This Life Is Not a Dress Rehearsal

The first step of the Visual Therapy process addresses what other make-over plans leave out or ignore: the *why* behind what holds us back, day after day, from looking our best.

It is nearly impossible to reinvent yourself without establishing a benchmark, your fashion square one, so to speak. That's what the first step of the Visual Therapy process is all about. Think of it as a reality check. Sure, it'd be nice to have the kind of lifestyle that warranted wearing Prada every day, but if you are an undergrad or grad student on a budget, or a stay-at-home mom who spends most of her day hustling the kids from nursery school to the park, does it really make sense for you to wear a cream cashmere dress? On the other hand, does wearing pilled sweatpants and your husband's old flannel shirt really make you feel good about yourself?

Warning Signals

Think about it. How many times a day are you bombarded by messages on television and radio, in print and in movies, over the Internet or on billboards, implying that in order to truly be successful or happy you must look either like a movie star or someone who spends her entire existence in the gym, drinking wheatgrass for breakfast, indulging on a lettuce leaf for lunch, and enjoying a sensible breath mint for dinner? We're conditioned by this bombardment of media hype to believe that if only we looked a certain way (tall, skinny, glamorous, and young), total happiness and the perfect life could be ours (and for 20 percent off!). Of course, no one can live up to such standards, so we end up resigned to defeat.

If this describes you, you may be experiencing emotional havoc, reinforced by the media, brought on by a psychological disconnect between your image and your identity.

How do we know this? As professional style consultants who have worked with countless women just like you, we know the major symptoms all too well. Maybe you feel like you have lost your vitality, or your style is flat. Maybe you're in the mood for a change, some inspiration, or are simply ready to take your style to the next level.

Failing to understand what image you are projecting through haphazard wardrobe choices affects how you are perceived by others.

When there is an incompatibility between style and a certain state of mind, it is never style that triumphs. —Coco Chanel (1893–1971), fashion couturiere

The Major Signs of Style Incompatibility

There are five major indicators of the disconnect between the outer you and the inner you, the result of an ill-defined (or perhaps never-defined) personal style. Recognize any of these symptoms? Rest assured, you have come to the right place for a remedy!

Sign #1: "I look and feel so dowdy these days!"

Many women experience this symptom when they go through major transitions in their lives, such as adjusting to marriage, motherhood (like Teri in the previous chapter), divorce, or a career change or promotion.

Whatever the transition in your life may be, the psychological and emotional fallout is the same. You see yourself in the mirror and think, *What happened?*

If you have kids, you may have what we affectionately dub the "Mom Clothes Syndrome." You've probably spent a good portion of time wearing clothes for their functionality only. How they made you look or, more important, *feel* about yourself was low on your list of priorities (if it made the list at all). In other words, you elevated function (comfort) over form (expression) as far as your wardrobe was concerned. The result? Your clothes are loose fitting and shapeless, uninspired and unflattering.

Because your top priority is taking care of your kids and your family (or your career, or all of the above), you've paid little or no attention to the obligation you have to take care of yourself. You begin to wonder whether you can feel sexy or beautiful anymore. You haven't taken the time to shop for clothes that are both functional *and* attractive, practical *and* luxurious (they *do* exist, you know), clothes that make you feel comfortable, confident, and alive.

Good news: Recognizing this symptom puts you on the road to recovery. As you work through the various exercises in this and the following Visual Therapy steps, you will come to understand that function and form aren't mutually exclusive. Rather than throw on any old thing in the morning just because it's there (and because it's easy), why not subscribe to a formula that helps you connect with a look that works for you, say, a pair of flattering, modern jeans (not too high, not too low) with a fun, form-fitting tee, or a cute, up-to-date track suit. A sporty look is perfect for running errands (you *are* running, after all).

*I was **not** ugly. I might never be anything for men to lose their heads about, but I need never again be ugly. This knowledge was like a song within me. Suddenly, it all came together: if you were healthy, fit, and well dressed, you could be attractive.* —Elsie De Wolfe (1865–1950), interior decorator

By putting just a bit of effort into defining your style (which is not only an important exercise but can also be a lot of fun) and reconnecting your identity with how you want others to see you, you can rid yourself of that dowdy alter ego in the mirror, and manage to look your best, no matter what the day may throw your way.

Beauty comes in many shapes, sizes, and ages.

Sign #2: "I feel so un–put together!"

Okay, it's ungrammatical, but you get the meaning. Clients who experience this symptom tell us their closets look like grab bags. They've got "tons" of clothes in there, many great-looking separates, each of which they like individually, but when it comes to putting an outfit together, nothing seems to work. The same woman could own a ballerina-style H&M skirt, a multicolored tweed Zara jacket, a chiffon floral ruffled blouse, animal-print pumps, a lavender sateen kick-pleat skirt from Banana Republic, not to mention a bunch of pastel satin-and-lace camisoles from Old Navy. Now, there's absolutely nothing wrong with mixing and matching fabrics, styles, and designers, but without some direction or vision, it can be a challenge to assemble a look that doesn't come off as schizophrenic.

If this sounds like you, maybe it's because you have a lot of "frosting" in your wardrobe—items that look fabulous and add a little stylish je ne sais quoi—but not enough "cake" (the basics, the foundation of your wardrobe) to support the statement you're trying to make. Then again, maybe it's the opposite: You've got a lot of solid cake but not enough frosting to top it off, and this makes you look and feel boring or flat. Either way, the resulting frustration you feel is the same.

The reason for a malfunctioning, mismatched, or discordant wardrobe is that you have either never defined your style or have not *re*defined it lately to uncover what it is *now*. This is more important than you might imagine: People evolve over time, just as fashion does.

Once you have defined your style, or redefined it, you will be able to edit your wardrobe accordingly, and fill in the gaps to pull together a complete look that clearly and authentically expresses the you that you want the world to see.

Sign #3: "I feel so fat!"

Welcome to America in the twenty-first century, a time when, statistics say, more than half of us are considered to be overweight. At the same time, we are assaulted by messages from the media telling us how svelte we should be. That's why many of us "feel fat" (we've all said it!) even if we are only a few pounds over our ideal weight.

We've had clients postpone their Visual Therapy until they managed to shed those extra pounds because they felt too Rubenesque to benefit from the process. If you're wondering whether you should go on a diet before embarking on this process, don't. Visual Therapy is about looking your best at your current weight, whether or not it changes in the near or distant future.

Most women in America admit to being at least one size larger than what they believe is their ideal weight. If you are one of them, keep reading. As you experience success with Visual Therapy you'll start seeing yourself looking great exactly as you are. "Feelin' it"—that is, feeling great, alive, and energized by the process—is the key to motivating yourself to stick with Visual Therapy. Once you commit to the process, you empower yourself to change many of the bad habits that got you in a rut in the first place. You'll begin to see possibilities everywhere.

Defining your style, an exercise based on who you are *now*, is the place to start ridding yourself of what we call the "I'm Fat Syndrome." When you complete this and the next two steps in the Visual Therapy process, you will have successfully cured yourself of the style blues.

Symptom: Shirley, a New Yorker, is a successful CPA in her forties. By her own admission, she loves sweets—cookies, brownies, the works. Every day in the late afternoon, Shirley feels the urge for a sugar fix. Unfortunately, her favorite bakery is next door to her office. Shirley claims that it's all but impossible to resist their delectable treats, and indulging gives her something to look forward to.

Prescription: After defining her style, completing her wardrobe edit, and filling in the gaps, Shirley—now looking and feeling great in one of her new put together looks—passes that bakery, sees the sweets beckoning, and, seeing her reflection in the glass, finds the willpower to resist. It's not easy, as she admits. But the first time she did this she called to tell us: "I walked right by and had a protein bar instead! I feel too good to just give in."

Outcome: Shirley saw the light called *possibility*, and she started buying clothes that were more flattering to her body, that emphasized her small waist (one of her best features). As a result, she looked slimmer and people thought she had lost weight. That lifted her spirits and, soon enough she did lose weight. She started going for a walk every morning before work to get in more exercise, no longer self-conscious but self-confident. She began dating again, and living her life more fully, all as a consequence of how great she felt looking her best *as herself today*.

Sign #4: "I feel as though maybe my old formula isn't working for me anymore."

If it occurs to you to ask this question, you're right—it probably isn't. After all, people change, styles change, times change. Over time, our faces change and so do our bodies. We change jobs, we change apartments or houses, we begin and end relationships, so why wouldn't our look change?

Change is natural. Change is good. Have you ever seen a woman who, from behind, looked like a teenager, long blond hair down to her waist, wearing a Juicy Couture sweatsuit . . . and when she turned around, you saw that she was actually in her fifties? The fact that her body looked good from the rear is certainly a compliment . . . but that hair! And that outfit!

Just because having long, thick, blond hair defined her look back in the 1970s, just because someone complimented her on her look back *then* doesn't mean that it works for her now. It's not age appropriate. Unaware of the time warp she's slipped into, she likely tells herself, "If it ain't broken, don't fix it." But it is broken. The formula needs fixing—or, to be more precise, it needs *reinventing*.

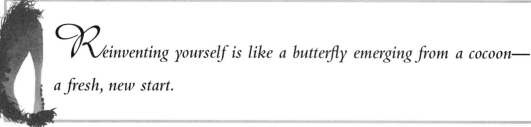

Reinventing yourself is like a butterfly emerging from a cocoon— a fresh, new start.

The fact of the matter is that even if you are consistent in your personal style, you may need to occasionally update your formula in order to reinvigorate that style. Life transitions occur on average about every five years. For example, first you graduate from high school and maybe enter college. That's one change. Then, after school, you embark on a career, or perhaps get married (or both)—that's another. Maybe you have kids—yet another. Before you know it, your kids are graduating from kindergarten . . . then middle school . . . then high school! Life moves forward, and as we move with it we take on new challenges and responsibilities. Reinventing your style throughout your life—sometimes a tweak, sometimes a tune-up—begins with redefining who you are, and where you are in the world.

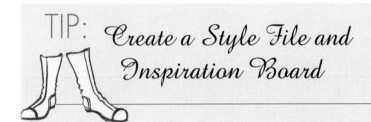

TIP: Create a Style File and Inspiration Board

One way to keep up on what's new is to look through fashion and lifestyle magazines such as *Harper's Bazaar*, *InStyle*, *Vogue*, *O* magazine, or *Lucky* for ideas and inspiration. The idea is to translate what you see in these magazines into looks that are appropriate *for you*—a process that will help you stay current and up to date. Write down your ideas or clip the pictures out and put them in a folder. Call it your ongoing style file. You can also post your favorites seasonally on a bulletin board to create a collage of looks that will serve as further inspiration.

Sign #5: "I don't need to look good every day!"

This is the ultimate symptom of resignation, an expression of completely giving in to the style blues. For example, a woman may tell us that because she leads a very low-key lifestyle, works at home, and doesn't get out much, she doesn't feel the need to dress up. "After all," she will say, "who sees me?"

You see *you*, every day! And Visual Therapy is not about dressing up, it's about becoming your personal best. The self you see in the mirror in the morning, in the window at the bank, on line at the deli, will affect how you feel about yourself, and about life in general, all day long.

Think about it. We've all overslept before, right? And you know that feeling, when you start the day rushing around frantically? It sets the tone for everything that follows.

It's the same with style. If you throw on any old thing in the morning because you think no one will see you, you are, in effect, going into hiding, particularly from yourself. How do you think this will impact the rest of your day, and affect those around you? On the other hand, if you got up twenty minutes earlier in the morning and took that time to make yourself look better *for you* by putting together an outfit that was flattering, you set yourself up to feel good. You create the potential to have a better and more fulfilling day.

Putting together a look that makes you feel your best doesn't mean you have to glam yourself up for a casual day at the office, or to get the kids off to school, or that you have to vacuum your house in a dress like June Cleaver. It means putting in as much effort as you need to create your unique look. If that look is jeans and a sweater, that's fine. But choose jeans and a sweater that are fitted and contemporary, rather than baggy and unstructured, so that you don't disappear in them.

Resigning yourself to look "good enough" because there's "no one to impress" during the course of a day means you have lost any motivation to look your best. Redefining your fashion personality is critical to achieving your own, unique style. It is also what motivates you to change, refine, and refresh your lifestyle to reflect who you are or who you want to be.

One of the keys to great style is owning your look.

Making a Diagnosis

There you have it, the five major indicators of style incompatibility—signals that tell you your look and your life are out of whack because your image and your identity are out of sync. The more symptoms you identify, the more disconnected things are.

So, how do you determine the nature and degree of that disconnect—the main impediment to your expressing your unique style? And what can you do to align your image and identity? First, you will need to gain, or regain, clarity about your personal style through two exercises. The first helps you to define your image, the second helps you to define your identity. Taken in tandem, the results of these exercises will help you determine how much of a disconnect you are faced with.

After completing these exercises, you will have a much better handle on your personal style, and greater understanding of the wardrobe most appropriate to you. You'll also possess the focus you will need to complete the rest of the Visual Therapy process.

Authentic style is achieved through the union of the external (your image) with the internal (your identity).

Defining Your Personal Style

Exercise #1: Define Your Image

To get to the root of the disconnect between your image and your identity, we start by profiling your image. This profile includes your current age and body type, your present lifestyle, and your living circumstances. You'll start thinking about your personal image, and encouraging you to determine what your style is (or what you perceive it to be). To simplify this exercise, we have defined the five general styles to which nearly all of us can relate.

Your image is what you want others to see. Your identity is who you are inside. Your image should be honest and true, a powerful aesthetic translation of the core values that make up your identity.

DEFINE YOUR AGE AND BODY TYPE

Age-appropriate wardrobe choices are essential to having great style. It is absolutely life-affirming to feel like you're twenty, even though you're forty, but that doesn't mean you should dress like you're twenty!

Similarly, acknowledging and accepting the reality of one's body type are important factors in achieving the best look for you. We've all bought clothes on impulse, impractical things that we snapped up because we fell in love with them on the spot, even though they may not be the most flattering to our body type (unless we lose those last few pounds!).

As hard as it is to resist such impulse purchases, and to resist being influenced by fashion trends into buying something inappropriate, you must try. If a below-the-knee skirt flatters the shape of your body and your legs more than a miniskirt, be honest with yourself. Skip the miniskirt. You'll save money and feel better about yourself and your purchase. As you will learn in Visual Therapy Step #2 (Edit Your Wardrobe), by sticking with choices that are most flattering to your body type and appropriate to your age, you will always be in style. To get you moving in the right direction, let's start with a reality check. The reason we ask you to clarify your age, body type, lifestyle, and arena in this exercise is to encourage you to accept the realities of your life and bring these factors to the fore when defining your style.

A. What is your age group? (check one):

- ☐ twenty-something
- ☐ thirty-something
- ☐ forty-something
- ☐ fifty-something
- ☐ sixty-something
- ☐ seventy-something

B. What is your body type? (check one):

- ☐ straight
- ☐ curvy
- ☐ full

Because women come in all shapes and sizes, some can be a combination of full *and* curvy.

DEFINE YOUR LIFESTYLE

Clarifying your lifestyle—your *present* lifestyle, not a past or projected one—is another essential ingredient in defining your image and making the right wardrobe choices. For example, a CEO's image is much different from that of a stay-at-home mom or a student.

What is your lifestyle? (check one):

- ☐ student
- ☐ stay-at-home mom
- ☐ working/professional
- ☐ CEO/entrepreneur
- ☐ philanthropist
- ☐ retired

DEFINE YOUR ARENA

Common sense dictates that dressing in a way that is appropriate to your environment and circumstances has as much to do with the image you project as does dressing appropriately for your age. Someone who lives in the country will obviously have different clothing requirements than someone who lives in a metropolitan area. If you happen to live in two or more arenas or climates, it would make your life a lot simpler to have pared-down wardrobes lined up in each location. What makes you feel comfortable and appropriate in one region

(and suitable for the climate), you might not wear in another. (Think about it: Santa Fe vs. Palm Beach vs. Boston, for example.) A woman who wears a Dolce & Gabbana suit in New York City might head to Miami each summer and feel more at ease in a brightly printed, flowing Roberto Cavalli skirt, paired with a tank top—a combo that goes better with the tropical weather and the Latin beat! After completing the Visual Therapy process, you will find that while your closets in various locales contain different pieces, they will still reflect your defined style.

What is your arena? (check one):

- ☐ country life
- ☐ suburbanite
- ☐ urban dweller
- ☐ traveler (multiple or seasonal homes)

DEFINE YOUR STYLE TYPE

After working with hundreds of people from coast to coast, we have come to the conclusion that each of us belongs to one or a combination of the following five style types:

- ➤ Classic
- ➤ Chic
- ➤ Whimsical
- ➤ Bohemian
- ➤ Avant-garde

Exercise #2: Define Your Style

Read each question carefully. There are no right or wrong responses. Simply take an honest impression of yourself. Be straight with yourself as you consider your answers, but don't think too hard or overanalyze. Trust your first impulse. Your first inclination is the one that will most honestly and accurately reflect your psychological and emotional fashion personality—i.e., your "internal" style, or the real you.

For accuracy in scoring, be sure to answer every question. Don't ignore any, or skip over one with the idea of coming back to it later after weighing your response some more. You may forget to come back to it and throw your score out of whack.

When you're done with the quiz, check the answer key on page 36 to see how you scored; then find out what the results mean.

THE VISUAL THERAPY STYLE QUIZ

This quiz is designed to point out your dominant style identity, the real you. Circle your response.

1. If we opened your closet, what color palette would we mostly see?

    a) black and neutrals

    b) basics, such as navy, white, khaki, charcoal, or brown

    c) earth tones

    d) a rainbow of colors

    e) black with touches of bold color

2. How would your friends describe you?

    a) playful and spirited
    b) relaxed and liberal
    c) sharp and direct
    d) traditional and proper
    e) innovative and forward-thinking

3. Given a choice, which would you rather do?

    a) throw on a pair of jeans, T-shirt with funky accessories
    b) step out in a fun floral dress or bright mixed prints
    c) put on a sleek V-neck top and modern-cut pant
    d) grab your favorite jacket with interesting and unusual details to wear with a black pant
    e) get comfortable in khakis, a collared shirt, and your cutest loafers

4. If someone gave you $200 for clothes, how would you use it?

    a) spend it on a cashmere wrap
    b) buy a couple of outfits at J.Crew or Banana Republic
    c) add to your accessories collection with a slouchy suede bag
    d) buy a dress that makes you feel smart and unique
    e) splurge on anything that catches your eye

5. When you walk into a crowded room, what would you prefer to do?

    a) stand out
    b) blend in
    c) be in control, exude power

d) seem natural and easygoing

e) be zany and animated

6. *When you have the urge (or need) to go shopping, you are more likely to do which of the following?*

a) purchase practical basics for all seasons

b) head to the flea market for some great "lived-in" and funky finds

c) get something with a splash of color to brighten your day

d) find that unusual piece to add to your wardrobe that no one else will have

e) buy high-quality, smart pieces that are sure to be in style

7. *When you flip through the pages of fashion magazines, what is most likely to catch your eye?*

a) that little black dress in the "special occasion" section

b) peasant blouses and denim

c) multicolored bangles for spring

d) a story on the new designers from Tokyo and Belgium

e) a Ralph Lauren lifestyle ad

8. *Which of the following best describes the decor of your home?*

a) minimalist, architectural, and sculptural (think the Jetsons)

b) comfortable and traditional (think the Cleavers)

c) fun, kitschy, and unorthodox (think *Alice in Wonderland*)

d) lots of rugs, earth tones, and floral prints (think 70s)

e) streamlined, tonal, with clean surfaces (think Tom Ford)

ANSWER KEY

How'd you do? The letter you circled reflects your *dominant* style identity as revealed by your answer to that question. Tally the number of times your response reflected Classic, Chic, Whimsical, Bohemian or Avant-garde in the space provided. The high score represents your *dominant* style identity, your *true* fashion personality; the second highest score could indicate your combination style.

1. a) Chic   b) Classic   c) Bohemian   d) Whimsical   e) Avant-garde

2. a) Whimsical   b) Bohemian   c) Chic   d) Classic   e) Avant-garde

3. a) Bohemian   b) Whimsical   c) Chic   d) Avant-garde   e) Classic

4. a) Chic   b) Classic   c) Bohemian   d) Avant-garde   e) Whimsical

5. a) Avant-garde   b) Classic   c) Chic   d) Bohemian   e) Whimsical

6. a) Classic   b) Bohemian   c) Whimsical   d) Avant-garde   e) Chic

7. a) Chic   b) Bohemian   c) Whimsical   d) Avant-garde   e) Classic

8. a) Avant-garde   b) Classic   c) Whimsical   d) Bohemian   e) Chic

Total Classic: _____

Total Chic: _____

Total Whimsical: _____

Total Bohemian: _____

Total Avant-garde: _____

Your Dominant Style at a Glance

Classic. Simple, clean, and traditional; a timeless look because the silhouette and colors rarely change. Always ladylike, classic garments are often tailored.

Chic. This style is defined by a powerful look and sharp lines that seem to come together in an effortless way. It is often monochromatic and combined with bold accessories.

Whimsical. This playful style appears to be "thrown together" but is actually a thoughtful combination of colors and patterns. The wearer is often young at heart and the look is sometimes ethereal and romantic.

Bohemian. Relaxed, lived-in, hippy or funky, incorporating offbeat accessories and usually lots of denim and suede. A relaxed look with an emphasis on natural fabrics and earth tones, this style evolved from the hippie look of the 1960s and early 1970s.

Avant-garde. This is an ultramodern style that uses fashion as an extension of the wearer's creativity. It often seeks to make a dramatic statement. Typically, the foundation for this wardrobe is black.

Read and consider the following profiles of each style type to determine which one (or more than one) you feel most closely reflects how you see yourself—that is, the image you are aiming for and want to project. Before you edit your closet—and especially before you hit the stores and spend money—it is important to have complete clarity on your defined style(s).

Annette   Classic

Classic

Meet Annette, an attractive young New Yorker in her mid-thirties. Annette works out of her home, a stylish, comfortable one-bedroom on the city's Upper West Side. She's organized a small corner of her living room into a well functioning but unobtrusive home office where she does freelance writing for many different types of magazines, ranging from financial trade publications to travel periodicals.

Annette has reached a point in her life where she has created a solid professional foundation for herself and her future. She recently became engaged to Brad, a financial adviser, and will soon be making the transition to married life. Everything about Annette speaks "traditional," "tasteful," and "in control," including her look, which is simple and clean. She chooses clothes and accessories of excellent quality (so they will last) with classic lines that endure and will always be in style—straight pant legs, for example, never flared, pegged, or cropped, no matter how often the styles may change.

Annette is a Classic. She goes for the conservative, the neat, and the timeless. Basic colors, such as navy, charcoal, and black-and-white, make up the cake of her wardrobe, while pastel accents (the frosting) add a nice feminine touch.

A size 6 to 8, Annette's everyday style consists of a flattering combination of Levi jeans paired with a fitted scoop-neck sweater, or a white collared shirt and a blazer with classic loafers on days when she's not having an important meeting, and an "Audrey shape" dress with strappy neutral leather heel for an event. She also uses a pair of simple diamond stud or pearl necklaces, a clean, simple, elegant watch, and a quality, leather handbag that go with all her outfits to pull her Classic look together.

The image projected by the Classic type, like Annette, makes a soft-spoken but confident statement that says, "I know where I'm going." A Classic focuses on the long range, but will never stray too far. She lets her solid foundation work for her, to take her where she wants to be, confident that it has staying power.

Classic icons:

Laura Bush
Katharine Hepburn
Grace Kelly
Diane Sawyer
Princess Diana (earlier years)
Renée Zellweger

Chic

Margaret is married to a successful attorney, and is the mother of a grown son. She keeps busy by sitting on the board of two museums and doing volunteer work with children for UNICEF at a nearby hospital. As she attends many fund-raisers and luncheons, she likes her outfits to say she is hardworking, social, but also in control. Margaret prefers to dress monochromatically, and she uses bold-statement accessories to complete her look. For example, with a chocolate-brown jersey knee-length dress, she may wear brown pumps and use an alligator handbag as the finishing touch to pull her look together. She looks amazing at every occasion and seems to do so effortlessly. A Chic is always seamlessly put together, and never overdone, but unlike a Classic she will add or combine stylish accessories to give her a sleek, modern, look—not necessarily considered timeless, perhaps, but always in perfect taste.

A Chic will go for clean, sleek lines, but will integrate a hint of the untraditional and the "now" into her outfit to create a personal look.

A Chic also prefers to keep her foundation outfit simple and elegant, but is more interested in—and therefore up on—what is current, although she is absolutely not a slave to the latest trends. She likes being fashionable but with a subtle flair that keeps the look uniquely hers.

A Chic like Margaret uses fashion as a tool to command respect in every situation. Even if, when attending a symphony concert, she is wearing a simple pair of modern charcoal trousers with a beautiful white organza blouse with a wide alligator belt, she will incorporate a vintage clutch, a fabulous pearl drop earring, and a simple shoe that blends effortlessly, rather than distracting from her overall look. The message? Confident, cool, and sophisticated, and very put together.

Chic icons:

Halle Berry
Catherine Deneuve
Audrey Hepburn
Carolina Herrera
Nicole Kidman
Jacqueline Kennedy Onassis

Whimsical

Georgia is an interior designer in her late forties, recently divorced, with one daughter who has just graduated from Northwestern University. Very much a free spirit, she recently sold her house in the suburbs on an impulse, and moved to the exciting city of Chicago where she bought a downtown loft to begin a new phase of her life.

Georgia approaches her wardrobe joyfully, like a hobby. She is an extremely visual person, youthful in attitude and appearance (a reflection of her newfound freedom). This essence shines through her wardrobe choices, where her use of color patterns and playful accessories expresses her whimsical nature. Everything about a Whimsical's look appears to be freewheeling, thrown together, a little "out there," but in reality is well planned and age appropriate.

Although you might not expect it, her foundation is composed generally of earth tones so that her funky accessories get center stage.

For running errands on spring weekends, she will wear a pair of khakis rolled up to mid-calf and a jean jacket, but step up her look with a colorful tee, and a floppy hat. Georgia has a great knack for mixing colors and patterns in a versatile and animated way so that her look is always changing—contemporary, sometimes flirtatious and sexy, and sometimes a little retro, but always playful and fun. By not taking her style too seriously, she is able to utilize a broad mix-and-match flexibility in her wardrobe, jazz up the practical in a funky or retro way, and turn her look up or down a notch so that she looks great no matter where she goes.

LAWRENCE LUCIER/GETTY IMAGES

Whimsical icons:

Mischa Barton
Sofia Coppola
Kirsten Dunst
Betsey Johnson
Vanessa Paradis
Gwen Stefani

Bohemian

Lori is a single mom in her mid-thirties with a four-year-old son. They live in Florida where she and her sister own and operate a small neighborhood health food store. The Bohemian style she prefers says hip, modern and funky—but in an organic, earthy way.

Lori's pre-pregnancy look was pure, resort-style Bohemian—full-on tie-dyed skirts; sexy, form-fitting T-shirts; flip-flops or sandals; a kind of sexy peasant style inspired by the seventies. Now that she's a mom, she wants a more sophisticated version of her old Bohemian formula, one better suited to her new lifestyle and responsibilities. So, she has traded in her tie-dyed skirts and tight T-shirts, and is refining her "hippie look" using flared jeans and trousers with funky jackets and offbeat accessories (such as Indian-inspired earrings and ethnic necklaces and cuffs) and a lot of denim and suede. Incorporating fabrics and textures that are warm and natural to the eye, her revised Bohemian style is a more sophisticated look than bottom-line hip. And because she lives in Florida, the look works well with the climate and the vibe.

Bohemian icons:

Kate Hudson
Jade Jagger
Ali MacGraw
Sienna Miller
Kate Moss
Stevie Nicks
Joss Stone

With easily tossed hair and a laid-back approach to life, Bohemians like Lori are saying to the world: "I am confident and comfortable in my persona, easygoing and relaxed, but still put-together."

Avant-garde

Six months pregnant, Natalie is a sculptor in her early thirties, living in Los Angeles, California, with her husband, Josh. Before her pregnancy, she was not afraid to wear a tuxedo pantsuit out to a cocktail party, and always found herself heading straight for the one stand-out item of clothing on a rack, such as a skirt with an asymmetrical hemline. Or, if she was going out to dinner with Josh, she'd throw on a Balenciaga sleeveless knee-length black dress with a thick belt, and pair it with a chunky "mod" heel. She goes for what some might describe as an *artsy* look—clothes that are almost beyond fashion, using art and intellect as the basis of an outfit. This is what the Avant-garde style is all about: making a statement that translates as, "I'm different—I'm not a fashion victim."

Natalie hasn't had to succumb to the dreaded "pregnancy ensembles," because her foundation has typically been all black or all brown anyway. All she felt the need for was to purchase a few more looser and easier tops and bottoms, and to mix them with jackets by Comme des Garcons, Yojhi, and A. Demeulemeester (all brands that focus on fashion-forward details), and this has done the trick for her! Her rule on how to approach pregnancy clothes has been "Don't buy anything unless you would love it even if you weren't pregnant."

Natalie is not an extreme Avant-garde, like, for example, the singer Bjork, who wore a notorious "swan dress" at the Oscar ceremonies some years back. Although part of the art world, Natalie would never go to such extremes in her look because she is a professional, and while she loves her Avant-garde image, she wants everyone to know that she has both feet firmly on the ground. She will go out on a fashion limb just far enough to maintain her uniqueness, but not so far as to look "costumey."

The Avant-garde style really can work for women who are pregnant, as it enables moms-to-be to wear clothes of varying shapes, sizes, and details that take attention away from, rather than directing it toward, her expanding maternal waistline.

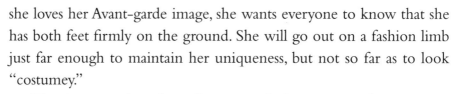

Avant-garde icons:

Björk
Cate Blanchett
Marlene Dietrich
Greta Garbo
Diane Keaton
Annie Lennox

DAVE HOGAN/GETTY IMAGES

Not All One or the Other?

Okay, what if your score is not so clear-cut? Say, for example, you scored mostly Classic but circled a couple of items that indicate you have Chic leanings. Or, what if your score doesn't perfectly jibe with the description? Does this mean you have an even bigger disconnect? No.

What it means is that most people are not all one type or all another but typically a combination of types, who express a different aspect of themselves at certain times in various areas of their lives.

For example, a person might be more Chic on weekends and more Classic during the week. When going to dinner on a Saturday evening, she may wear a sexy black pant, slightly flared, a fitted white shirt, a cashmere wrap, a sleek black clutch, high-heeled pumps, diamond studs, and a silver cuff—a Classic foundation but with Chic details, like the slight flare in the pant, the cuff, and the clutch, the combination of which says Classic/Chic. But at work or a business luncheon, she may prefer a pair of heels, a slim skirt and cashmere sweater, or pants with a classically tailored jacket.

Classic/Chic (or, if you prefer, Chic/Classic) is, in fact, a very common combination of style types. Here are some others:

► *Whimsical/Chic.* This combo enjoys adding a whimsical dash of color to a Chic look of modern elegance. For example, she might wear a three-quarter-length jersey black dress in a luxurious fabric (a monochromatic foundation piece), but throw a multicolored print jacket, or add Bakelight jewelry, big sunglasses, and/or a colorful scarf to project a look that is both Whimsical *and* Chic.

► *Avant-garde/Chic.* This mixture works particularly well. Think back to our description of the Avant-garde style and the profile of Natalie: The Avant-garde/Chic is someone who moves back and forth between these two style types as needed, so that she is more approachable. Incorporating one Avant-garde piece—a pair of modern jodphur trousers, or a blazer with an asymmetrical zipper closure instead of the traditional two-button or three-button blazer—will give you just the right Avant-garde edge without looking loony! It will add interest and still look sophisticated.

➤ *Bohemian/Chic.* Lori, the Bohemian-turned-Chic described in our "Bohemian" profile, is a prime example of this combination. While remaining true to her Bohemian roots, now that she is an adult with a busy lifestyle and lots of responsibilities she downplays her Bohemian side for a more sophisticated Chic look that better reflects the woman she is today (but always with that unexpected funky touch).

Never the Two Shall Meet

Avant-garde/Classic. Here's a combination you will likely never see. The Classic woman is not interested in making a dramatic statement about herself because it directs too much attention to her personal style, something she does not want. Conversely, the Avant-garde woman is completely confident in her style, and doesn't care what people think.

What It All Means

If the image you picked for yourself in Exercise #1 matches the identity you most related to in Exercise #2, does this mean you have no psychological disconnect and are therefore 100 percent in sync with your personal style? Not necessarily, or you wouldn't have any sense of the style-incompatibility symptoms you identified earlier. What it does mean is that the disconnect you are experiencing might be caused by a transition in your life.

Let's say, for example, that you are beyond a shadow of a doubt a Classic, and this is the look you want to project (and you do). But you have recently retired—is it still a good fit? Of course it is—while Classic for work looks different than home/casual Classic, it is still Classic.

On the other hand, perhaps the profile you chose in Exercise #1 and the identity you reflected in Exercise #2 are entirely different. This can happen, too. Consider the following:

Symptom: Debbie is entering the workforce as an account executive in a major manufacturing firm in Atlanta. Having spent the last four years in college, Debbie's closet reflects that phase of her life; her wardrobe consists of T-shirts, jeans, tank tops, and a vintage suede jacket—all very Bohemian—but nothing appropriate for her first big job. Although she selected Bohemian in Exercise #1, she scored Classic in Exercise #2 because she is changing her lifestyle.

Prescription: Debbie now defines her style as Classic because she wants to project a professional image in light of her new role, but she doesn't want to sacrifice energy and interest. She wants her new Classic look to express her youthful and slightly romantic side as well.

On close examination of her wardrobe during the editing process (which we'll describe in Step #2), she found that mixed in with all those tees and tank tops she did have a few basics that could be adapted to a Classic style: a black turtleneck, for example, plus a flirty skirt, a navy blazer, and a pair of black flats. She developed her plan of attack for filling in the gaps and pulling her new look together. Compiling a list of critical needs, items that could be combined with her edited wardrobe, she knew what was needed to give her enough outfits to start off with until she gets her first paycheck. This list consisted of a white blouse, a pair of classic black pants, a traditional black skirt, and a pair of black leather pumps (which she later found at an outlet mall for a steal).

Outcome: Debbie was able to pair the new white blouse and pumps with her flirty skirt to create Outfit #1; her black turtleneck and black pants or skirt with her black flats to create Outfits #2 and #3; and her white blouse under a navy blazer along with the pair of jeans (for dress-down day at work) to create Outfit #4. *Voilà!* Debbie had successfully evolved her personal style, creating a new look appropriate for the beginning of her new life. This is a very basic beginning, but it's a good start. She will later spice things up with great hair and makeup and a few accessories with color. She will build on this further by adding more great basics in other classic colors.

Debbie will not lose her Bohemian roots; instead, she reserves it for weekends and evenings. Debbie is now a Classic/Bohemian.

A constant style is a consistent thread that weaves through your life but is "tweaked" as you evolve. Having a constant style allows you to be more focused and sure in your way of dressing.

Lay Out a Style Statement

Now that you've got a clear, up-to-date picture of your personal style, it's time to create a road map for achieving it. Take the file you are filling with ideas and pictures for inspiration, and jot down the following:

1. The style or combination of styles that BEST DESCRIBE who you are the MAJORITY of the time. The one you scored the highest goes first. Choose from among the following alternatives: Classic; Chic; Whimsical; Avant-garde; Bohemian; Classic/Chic; Whimsical/Chic; Avant-garde/Chic; Bohemian/Chic, or your own combination.

2. The words or phrases you feel BEST DESCRIBE how you want to be perceived by others at this current stage of your life. Don't censor yourself. Use as many words or phrases as you like. Be as thorough as you can, and as with your responses to Exercise #2, don't be afraid to go with the first words or phrases that pop into your mind. Some examples: "Put-together," "easygoing and relaxed," "sexy," "intelligent," "in charge," "quiet and understated," "beautiful," "authentic," "creative," "reliable," and so on.

3. The names of some celebrities or persons in your own life whose personal style you especially admire (for example, Jackie O, Grace Kelly, Halle Berry, Cate Blanchett, your sister or coworker) because they dress in a way that is appropriate to their age and body type, lifestyle, and environment, and is true to their fashion personality or style type. This is to help inspire your own style, not influence you into emulating someone else's. You may choose from among the representative icons we suggested for each type or, better yet, come up with your own

inspirational figures. For example, one of our clients, a doctor, identified Kristen Davis's style in her role as Charlotte from *Sex and the City* as one she especially admires because it projects such self-confidence and femininity.

Now, take this information and combine it with your responses in Exercise #1 to lay out your complete style self-portrait in one concise statement (see Figure 1).

Figure 1. My Style Statement

My age group is: _____

My body type is: _____

My lifestyle is: _____

My arena is: _____

The personal style that describes me best now is: _____

I want others to perceive me now as the following because these words best describe the image I wish to portray: _____

I admire and am inspired by the personal style of [select *one* from your style file]:

_____

When you have completed your style statement, photocopy it or clip it out and tack it to a bulletin board or the inside of your closet. Put it where you will be able to access it quickly and refer to it easily throughout the rest of the Visual Therapy process. It will help keep you focused and motivated. At the conclusion of the Visual Therapy process, you'll put your style statement in the "style file" you will create in Step #5, as a way of keeping the inspiration flowing and steadily nurturing the new you.

Inspiration is the foundation on which the "optimum you" will be built.

Change Your Look, Change Your Life

Meet Stephanie, a striking African American woman who is a successful partner at a Chicago law firm.

Symptom: Stephanie sought out Visual Therapy because she felt that in order to further her career she needed to change the image she projected to her fellow partners, the staff, and business associates of the firm, a group made up largely of men.

Stephanie

Classic-Chic

R.T.

Stephanie felt she was perceived more often than not as a young associate, rather than the competent lawyer and partner she is. She wanted to walk into the firm's conference room confidently projecting a commanding and "in charge" presence that exuded power. She was searching for the pieces to the puzzle that would pull her look together and send that message. Because she had already spent a great deal of money on her clothes but had not achieved the desired effect, she contacted us.

Prescription: We told her that in order to look the part, she also had to *feel* the part. Stephanie had a fairly well-defined fashion personality. Her taste was on the Classic side—perhaps too much so, since she was looking to command the spotlight and not stand by the sidelines. The solution we devised while working with her was for her to add a strong element of Chic to her style. We had noticed some Chic undertones already in her look—she was a Classic/Chic, understated but also powerful—and the Chic part of the puzzle was underutilized in her look, thereby muting her message.

With a crowded work schedule typical of a top lawyer, Stephanie needed to be able to assemble her newly discovered Classic/Chic look quickly and in a way that would work immediately. She achieved this by combining those items of clothing in her closet that went well with her new Chic purchases. Her new work wardrobe consisted of:

➤ two complete Armani suits
➤ a pair of basic black pants
➤ a short black boot to give her pantsuits some height and attitude
➤ three blazers
➤ one pair of black heels to wear with skirts
➤ a high-quality tote

This may seem like an awfully small work wardrobe for a big-time lawyer, but with the flexibility she was able to achieve through coordination, Stephanie didn't need much more than that. By adding a perfect pair of silver drop earrings from Tiffany & Co., and investing in a beautiful watch, she instantly looked and felt authoritative and "in charge."

Outcome: Stephanie felt so empowered by her new Classic/Chic work wardrobe that she wanted to bring that style to her casual wardrobe, too. She returned to her closet for another round of editing (Visual Therapy Step #2), then shopped to fill in the gaps (Visual Therapy Step #3), and soon she had pulled together (Visual Therapy Step #4) a Classic/Chic casual wardrobe, all of it coordinated, enabling her to mix and match as her spirit and activities moved her.

Her casual wardrobe consisted of:

➤ three twinsets: black, brown, and coral.
➤ several knit tops in black, brown, and various colors with various necklines
➤ a pair of boot-cut, slightly low-rise jeans
➤ two pairs of casual pants (khaki and black)
➤ a modern short brown boot
➤ a sexy trench coat

The sense of empowerment Stephanie felt as soon as all the pieces of the puzzle were in place was immediate and apparent to everyone around her. She used her newfound confidence to further excel at work and was inspired to realize her full potential by improving her diet and exercising. She now commands respect in any room she enters—whether it is the firm's conference room or her favorite hangout.

You too can achieve what Stephanie has. With a deeper insight into your fashion personality achieved by having successfully defined your style *as it is now*, you are ready to tackle the next step in the Visual Therapy process. You are ready to move on to matching your world (and your closet) to your personal style—and bring rhyme and reason to your wardrobe choices and fashion purchases.

Edit Your Wardrobe

Seeing Is Believing

Just as the purpose behind defining your personal style is to achieve greater understanding and clarification of who and where you are in your life *now*, the purpose behind editing your wardrobe is to achieve "wardrobe clarity." Done correctly, it is a process of redefinition and renewal, not just cleaning out the clutter.

Wardrobe clarification will result in the elimination of that daily dose of dread you experience whenever you open your closet, peer into the abyss, and sigh, "I've got nothing to wear!" It is a process similar to that of getting rid of a lot of emotional baggage with the help of a good therapist, and will considerably reduce your level of stress throughout the day.

Editing your wardrobe is not about throwing things away needlessly, but "clarifying." It's about reading the clothing in your closet like tea leaves to find out what works, and establishing a life cycle for your wardrobe.

Hundreds of Visual Therapy clients agree: Editing your wardrobe will liberate you, because when you complete this step, you will have succeeded in:

➤ purging your closet of all that is inappropriate to the style you've defined

➤ organizing your closet to make it accessible to your everyday needs

➤ streamlining your wardrobe, so you will be able to quickly and easily pull together your style

➤ eliminating style difficulties by achieving wardrobe clarity

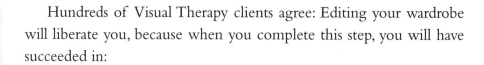

Your closet should be a Zen space to which you retreat in order to express yourself, not a torture chamber.

What You Will Need

Since you will be doing a love-it-or-leave-it edit of your entire wardrobe, preparation is vital. You don't want to have to stop midway to run out and get something you need in order to complete the task. If you stop and start, you may lose your mojo midstream. Enthusiasm is very important at this stage in order to keep momentum!

These are the supplies you will need to gather in advance and put in your Visual Therapy Wardrobe Survival Kit to successfully complete your edit. These items are easy to find (we'll give you pointers where); they won't cost you an arm and a leg; and you will get a lot of use out of them both during this step and afterward.

1. **Matching Hangers**

   These are essential for bringing clarity to your closet because uniform hangers keep your clothes at the same level, making it easier to view what you have, and, therefore, easier to get at. They create an aesthetic similar to having your own private boutique. This is important in reducing the visual clutter that contributes to the out-of-control feeling you get every time you open your closet door.

   ➤ *What to Buy*

   The simplest and most widely used hangers are clear or black plastic hangers with some form of grip or foam so that clothes do not slip. Wooden hangers look beautiful but they are costly (about $180 a box) as well as bulky. And, remember, you are going for streamlined and compact, not bulky or heavy. (For information on Visual Therapy Essential Hangers and Closet Accessories, consult our Web site, www.visual-therapy.com.)

   Wire hangers are a no-no. They sag under the weight of some garments and soon lose their shape, destroying the visually pleasing, eye-level consistency of your wardrobe arrangement. Even worse, they can leave wire marks on your clothes, and their sag can distort a garment's shape. This is not only bad for the clothes, but counterproductive to a major goal of Visual Therapy—being able to put together the right look, right away.

   We recommend getting a box of 100 plastic hangers with clips for skirts and pants; these will run you about $45 a box. Get another box of 100 hangers for shirts, which will cost about $65 a box. Two hundred hangers may strike you as a bit excessive at first, but you will soon discover, as most of our clients have, that you need more hangers than you ever expected. If it turns out that you require a few

extra, make do by scavenging extra hangers (of the same type) from elsewhere in your home or apartment rather than stopping to go out and buy more (unless, of course, that is the only alternative).

➤ *Where to Get It*

Any large department store, such as Wal-Mart, Target, K-Mart, Kohl's, California Closets, Home Décor, Boscov's, Sears, Hold Everything, and The Container Store. You can also go to www.visual-therapy.com and click on Essential Closet Accessories.

2. General Supplies

➤ *What to Buy*

A pad and pens for making notes to yourself as you go through the editing process. You will be determining which pieces are missing from your current inventory and/or will need replacing in order to put together different looks. You will need these notes for Step #3 when you go shopping to fill in the gaps.

Large plastic garbage bags for transporting the items you are discarding, as well as some labels or stickers for labeling each bag accordingly, in order to avoid any mix-ups about what's going where (charity, friends, or relatives). This is an important consideration if you wind up with lots of bags.

➤ *Where to Get It*

All of the above items are generally available at any well-stocked office supply store, drugstore, or supermarket.

3. Collapsible Rolling Rack

This type of rack will give you a reusable workstation, out of the way of your closet, for temporarily hanging items as you edit. It is a place to sort things in an organized way, as you break them down into different love-it-or-leave-it categories, making the clarification process go more smoothly.

➤ *What to Buy*

Be sure that the rack you choose is sturdy (made of thick, steel tubing) and that it is collapsible. As it will cost anywhere from $70 to $100 depending on the store and the dimensions of the rack (we recommend one that is at least 74½" x 2" x 67" high), you want it to be collapsible so that you can easily store it and, later, take it out again. You'll be using it again for future seasonal edits, for wardrobe clarification updates as you nurture the new you in Step #5, or for hanging clothes in canvas bags in your attic or basement, the items you may choose to "archive" as you get into the editing process.

➤ *Where to Get It*

Hold Everything. Stores are located in California, Florida, Massachusetts, Michigan, New York, and the District of Columbia. Online ordering is also available at www.holdeverything.com.

The Container Store. Thirty-three stores are located in twenty-one markets from coast to coast. Online ordering is also available at www.thecontainerstore.com.

All-in-One Suppliers. This is a Manhattan-based shopping resource for showroom furnishings, including racks, located at 223 West 35th Street, New York, NY 10001. Catalogue orders may be placed by phone; call 212-564-6240. Online ordering is not currently available but the company does have an e-catalogue on its site: www.allinonesuppliers.com.

4. **Full-Length Mirror**

If you do not already own one, this is an essential purchase for use during the editing process. Only by seeing how well each item in your closet fits you, how flattering (or unflattering) it looks on you from every angle, how it makes you feel to see yourself in the piece, and how well or poorly it suits your personal style will you be able to decide whether to love-it-or-leave-it.

Be sure you have good light near your mirror. If you have a walk-in closet of a reasonable size, where you can step back and see yourself fully, tack the mirror to your closet door. Three-way mirrors are great for seeing how you look from behind; a hand-held mirror is a good alternative if a three-way is not available.

➤ *What to Buy*
Recommended dimensions: 55" x 22". The cost can range from $20 to $150 for a hanging mirror of acceptable quality, depending on styling and decoration.

➤ *Where to Get It*
You can purchase inexpensive full-length mirrors at Wal-Mart; Kmart; Target; Bed Bath and Beyond, and cheval-type mirrors at major department or home furnishings store in your area.

How Long Will the Job Take?

The amount of time you will need to devote to the editing process will depend on the size of your wardrobe. Obviously, the more clothes you have to go through, the longer the edit will take.

The amount of time this step takes also will depend on how successfully you free yourself of interruptions, how well you can resist over-thinking your decisions and bogging yourself down, and how easily you can let go. Below are some tips on how to avoid these traps and pitfalls, and how to stay motivated and inspired to make it to the finish line.

Generally speaking, we have found that for most average-size closets wardrobe clarification takes about two days.

➤ **Day One.** For the love-it-or-leave-it edit; for organizing items you are keeping on shelves and hangers; and for bagging up items you are letting go.

➤ **Day Two.** For finishing the edit, following up after the edit, and storing or delivering the bags of discarded items to wherever they are going. Get them out of sight before you start second-guessing yourself!

Schedule as much time as you will need, whether it is the two days described above or more, blocks of time over a single day, or whatever. But apportion enough time for editing, and enough for follow-up. *And stick to your schedule.*

To avoid distractions, we urge you to turn off your cell phone and mute your answering machine while you are working.

TIP: *Get a Sitter*

We can almost hear you saying it: "Avoid interruptions? Sure, that's easy for you to say; you don't have two kids." True. But it is important that you treat each step in the Visual Therapy process (but especially this one because it is the most time-consuming) as *your* time. That means time you have carved out *for yourself* to come to terms with your closet and build a wardrobe that works for you. You won't be rid of interruptions if you do not *allow yourself* that free time. Remember: If you aren't good for you first, you can't be good for those around you.

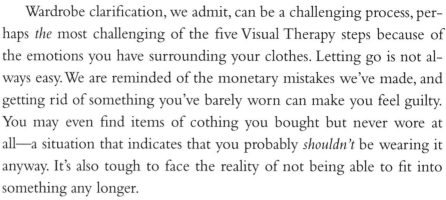

Wardrobe clarification, we admit, can be a challenging process, perhaps *the* most challenging of the five Visual Therapy steps because of the emotions you have surrounding your clothes. Letting go is not always easy. We are reminded of the monetary mistakes we've made, and getting rid of something you've barely worn can make you feel guilty. You may even find items of cothing you bought but never wore at all—a situation that indicates that you probably *shouldn't* be wearing it anyway. It's also tough to face the reality of not being able to fit into something any longer.

Remember that when you let something go, the time has come to make room for the new and updated version of it in your wardrobe. Completing this edit will be rewarding because the new you will start to emerge. So, keep your focus and don't get discouraged.

Just Wondering . . .

Wouldn't it be better to edit my wardrobe when it's cooler, or after I move? Procrastination is the thief of time. There is no ideal start date for wardrobe clarification. No, you don't have to launch into it five minutes after defining your style. But if you aren't feeling excited, motivated, and eager to apply yourself to this step, then maybe you should take a second look at your results in Step #1; perhaps you weren't as forthcoming and honest in your responses to some of the questions as you thought you were, because *something* is making you hesitate. You may need to go through Step #1 one more time and define your style again—more accurately this time—so you *will* be ready and eager to start editing. The sooner you start, the sooner you will begin to experience the life-changing results of Visual Therapy—wardrobe clarity and newfound confidence in your style as you make your way through the world.

Where Should You Begin?

If you feel overwhelmed by your closet when you open it to get dressed, you are probably going to feel twice as overwhelmed when you open it to tackle your wardrobe edit.

Many of our clients have told us that after defining their personal style and making the initial preparations to edit their wardrobe, they felt all fired up, *until* they opened the closet door. Then they felt confounded as to where and how to begin. That's why it is important to plan a strategy for editing upfront. Here is a system that will help you know where and when to start and will help get you through the process until it is completed.

For starters, create a Zen atmosphere by burning a candle, having flowers in the room, playing soothing music to help you relax. Drink plenty of water to stay hydrated. And open the curtains in the room so you can see. Sunlight brightens everything!

We suggest that you start at one end of your closet and move steadily toward the other. For single-level closets, we recommend going from left to right; for closets of two levels or more, move from left to right, starting with the top shelf, then come down to the next level—the core of your closet, containing your most active clothes (the items you wear most often). Then work your way down to the floor of your closet, where shoes and other accessories are placed; then to closet (or bedroom) drawers for T-shirts, undergarments, and any other accessory items that need editing.

If your closet is relatively small and your hanging clothes are crammed tightly together, you might want to take things out in portions rather than an item at a time, and put each portion temporarily on your collapsible rolling rack for a better view of what's there. Follow the same procedure with each batch you examine until you have reviewed them all.

Clarifying Your Wardrobe: The Three Qs

Be prepared to create four separate areas for your clothes and identify them as follows:

➤ my **"YES" area**—for "keeper" items, to be placed on new hangers and back into the closet
➤ my **"NO" area**—for items I am "letting go," piled neatly on the floor, to be bagged up
➤ my **"ALTERATIONS" area**—for salvageable items that might be flattering with some tweaking (i.e., dry cleaning, tailoring)
➤ my **"MAYBE" area**—for "I can't decide" items. *Use this only as a last resort! Re-ask yourself the questions that follow below and make a decision!*

Your closet tells a story, and to figure out the plotline, you need to see your wardrobe's heroes and its villains.

As you try on articles of clothing and accessories that are in question (as opposed to the items you will pull out and know right away what to do with them), and evaluate yourself in your full-length mirror, ask yourself the following love-it-or-leave-it questions, what we call "the three Qs," about each item:

1. Do I love it?
2. Is it flattering?
3. Does it represent me, and is this the image I want to portray?

Let's explore the three Qs in more detail.

Do I Love It? — To "love it" means that the garment or accessory truly inspires you and makes you feel amazing. For example, Jane loves her fabulous single-breasted black-and-white herringbone blazer because it meets many fashion needs. It breaks up her mostly black wardrobe and carries her from day to evening in an effortless way. She also loves it because she can dress it up as a suit with white or black trousers, or down with jeans and a tee and wear the blazer as a jacket on a casual evening, or with other tops.

Sophie was in her favorite vintage store in New York City recently and spotted a pair of very mod, late sixties, A. Courreges white mid-calf, flat-heel leather boots. They were snap-front with a patch detail on the heel. They looked terrific on her, and their flat heels make them very comfortable. The rounded toe and white color suited her Avant-garde style, and this is exactly the image she likes. She also loves them because they look great worn with jeans or skirts or even short A-line dresses and make more of a fashion statement than a classic pair of boots does. This gives her a lot of flexibility: She can wear these boots with almost anything, as they give anything she wears that "modern edge" she loves.

Is It Flattering? — An article of clothing is "flattering" when you are pleased with what you see when you look in the mirror. Why? Because how you respond to what you see is very likely how others will respond to what they see as well.

Clothes flatter because they accentuate the positive about you. Let's say you put on a sleeveless jersey dress with an empire waistline that is full at the bottom. You love the color, plum, but every time you move, your stomach is accentuated because jersey is not the most forgiving fabric. This may not be flattering. If you are uncomfortable wearing it, that will show—so leave it.

When you wear something that you know flatters you, you feel good wearing it, and, therefore, you project a feeling of confidence and well-being. A key strategy of Visual Therapy is for you to come away

Sophie

Avant-Garde

from the editing process feeling this way about everything in your wardrobe—because you will have put together an "optimal wardrobe" in which every item is flattering. This saves you from wasting a lot of time and energy each day trying to figure how to put together your desired "look." It will all work, all the time.

For example, when Brenda, a mother of two, looks in her full-length mirror, she thinks the pair of loose-fitting jeans she is trying on make her butt look larger than it really is, and that doesn't make her feel good. Leave it! But another pair of jeans she tries on, which is slightly low-rise (operative word: *slightly*) and boot-cut, makes her look shapely, not bottom heavy, giving her a feeling of being sexy and modern. This is obviously a flattering choice. Love it!

Does It Represent Me, and Is This the Image I Want to Portray? — The main objective of wardrobe clarification is to determine whether each piece of clothing in your closet sends the right message about you. Does it say what you want it to say about you in an appropriate way? That's why this third Q is so important. Is it possible for you to love an item and for it to be flattering, but also for that item to be inappropriate in some way and send the wrong message? Yes!

For example, Elizabeth, a cute redhead in her late twenties, had just taken a new job as an assistant editor at a women's magazine. Rifling through her closet for something to wear on her first day, she stopped at her multicolored jewel-tone paisley Etro chiffon shirt. The rope detailing around the neck and deep slit at center front neck, along with all the sequin and jewel embellishments, make it one of her most interesting and favorite tops. She would describe herself as Bohemian/Chic, so it definitely fits her defined style, and it looks perfect with her hair color. But since it is see-through, she is never quite sure what she should wear underneath (a nude cami?).

The next morning, in a panic, Elizabeth throws it on and opts for a nude bra and white jeans with chocolate-brown espadrilles, hoping the bra won't show. Much to her discomfort, however, she finds that when speaking with male associates, their gaze is not always focused on her face. Yes, the shirt flatters her; yes, she loves it; but it is not the image she wants to present at work. It is the perfect look for an evening out with friends, but excessive glitz and anything see-through should stay out of the office or professional daytime environment.

It is important to realize that no matter how much you love an item, how flattering it is on you, and how well it represents you, you must have a clear vision of where you are going in it. Sometimes we envision a certain lifestyle that isn't realistic. Samantha, a grad student and one of our New York City clients, purchased a heavily beaded ivory satin-based skirt from Matthew Williamson. It is gorgeous, but too formal for her college lifestyle, and when asked where she was going in that, we got a blank stare (and a laugh). She knew she got caught up in the moment with that purchase and had not kept her lifestyle in mind.

TIP: *Change Hangers as You Edit*

As you give each item the love-it-or-leave-it test, change the old hangers on things you are keeping. To jump-start the process of reorganizing your closet later, put skirts, shirts, pants, or jackets on your rolling rack in categories now, or back in your closet in groups. In addition to helping you keep things straight, this temporary arrangement will provide you with some instant gratification as you begin to see your wardrobe take shape, giving you the energy to keep on going.

Okay, now you are wondering what to do when an item gets a "no" to the last of the three Qs during the editing process but you still love it. If it is flattering, must it still go into the discard pile, even if it will work appropriately for a Saturday night? The answer is: no.

If this item represents the image you want to portray in another area of your life, then it is a "yes." It could represent the "resort" or "vacation" you, meaning it stays but should be moved to a "resort clothes" section of your wardrobe so that it won't take up valuable space in your active day-to-day wardrobe. Be careful, though; listen to your first instinct. There are other options, as you soon see.

What the Three Qs Will Tell You

As you ask of each item in your closet the three love-it-or-leave-it wardrobe clarification questions, your responses will determine one of the following courses of action.

An unqualified "yes" to all three questions determines that the item is a "keeper." It is one of the greatest-hit pieces in your present wardrobe because it works with your current style. These garments will go back in your main closet on matching hangers or on shelves because they are things you wear all the time—your active wardrobe.

An unqualified "no" to any of the three wardrobe clarification questions indicates that the item has to go. These are garments to be gotten rid of—parts of your past you should leave behind.

A garment that gets a "maybe" is one that you may have to come back to again at some point in the editing process because at the moment you can't make up your mind about it. When you return to it later, ask the three Qs again; you'll arrive at a decision much more easily this time, if it hasn't come to you already.

You will now have the "yes" clothes on your rolling rack and "no" clothes stacked in piles. Comparing the two batches, you can better see what your active wardrobe will look like, and this should make it easier to decide whether those "maybes" go in the "yes" or "no" column.

It's a good idea to merchandise your closet after the edit so every day you feel like you are shopping in your "personal boutique." Hang as much as possible—things can get lost in drawers. Organize hanging clothes by style (tanks, short-sleeve, long-sleeve, etc.) then by color (light to dark). Fold items following the same formula before you put them in drawers or on shelves.

The goal? A streamlined wardrobe composed of all your greatest hits.

Just Wondering . . .

What if I still can't make up my mind? Ask yourself the following Visual Therapy bonus questions: "When was the last time I wore it?" As a general rule, if your answer is twelve months ago or longer, the item belongs in the "no" pile. If this is the case, ask: "Why do I never reach for it?" The answer may be that you are simply tired of it and ready for something new. Last, but not least: "Where am I going to wear this?" Try to imagine a realistic situation where you would wear the piece. If you can't, it's a "no," too.

Letting Go

People hold on to clothes until they can no longer see what's in their closet, and for all sorts of reasons. Maybe they paid a lot of money for an item and their frugal side won't let them part with it, whether it's

Get inspired. Gather tear sheets from magazines, pictures, and any other things that inspire you to create your own inspiration board, a critical part of Step #1.

Ready for a change?
Julie's wardrobe and image did not represent the woman she had become.

Documentation. Taking pictures of optimal looks to create a personal look book saves you time and frustration when "pulling it together."

Casual/Weekend

Calvin Klein Ivory Lthr Jacket
Ivory Turtleneck
Charcoal Pinstripe Wool Pant
Black Suede Booty

Special Event Day

Ann Taylor Ivory/Blk Check Coat
Ivory Blazer and Tank
Black Wool Pant
Black Boots and Gloves

Evening

Armani Blk/Wht Lthr Blazer
Black Cashmere Camisole
Black Wool Pant
Black Booty

Business Day into Evening

Armani Blk/Wht Tweed Blazer
White Tank
Black Pencil Skirt
Prada Black Pumps

On-Camera/Speaking

Armani Red Cashmere Blazer
Black Tank
Black Wool Pant
Prada Black Pump

Cockt...

Valentino Black Dress
Black C Louboutin Heel
Diamond Studs

Your best foot forward. Julie's organized closet and updated look allow her to focus on what really matters in life.

Classic

Chic

RT

Whimsical

Bohemian

RT

Avant-Garde

R.T.

worn out, never worn, just doesn't work, or no longer fits. Or perhaps an item is like an old friend. It's been with them through thick and thin, and they're attached to it, for sentimental reasons, even though they haven't worn it for years. Or maybe they just feel uncomfortable about parting with any old clothes for fear of not finding or being able to afford anything new to replace them.

If you can get real with yourself and admit that you don't love that jacket, top, skirt, dress, pair of jeans—*whatever*—and/or it isn't flattering, there is no point in holding on to it, even if you have paid a lot of money for it. It will hang in the closet unworn, collect dust, take up valuable space, and become future clutter, making you feel even worse about the purchase every time you come across it.

Likewise, if you love it but it doesn't fit, there is no point talking yourself into putting it back in the closet in the event that someday it will fit you again. Deal with it *now*.

But what happens when an item may no longer look good on you and no longer fit, but has sentimental value? Or, maybe it looks good on you, but doesn't reflect your current style?

Depending upon the nature of the "no" that's given, there are three options for letting go: 1) Leave It; 2) Archive It; or 3) Demote It.

Leave It

Clearly if a garment has holes, is frayed, faded, or just plain "tired" looking, then to leave it means to throw it away. But in Visual Therapy, you can leave it in other ways, too.

If the garment is still in good condition and wearable but inappropriate to your present style, you can pass it on to a family member or friend who might enjoy having it, or donate it to a charity of your choice like the Salvation Army or Goodwill Industries, or perhaps a

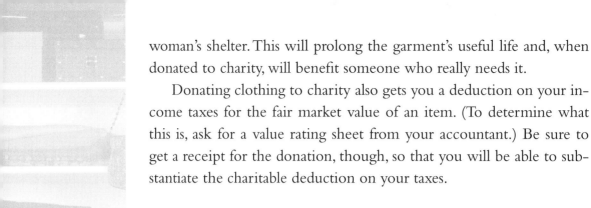

woman's shelter. This will prolong the garment's useful life and, when donated to charity, will benefit someone who really needs it.

Donating clothing to charity also gets you a deduction on your income taxes for the fair market value of an item. (To determine what this is, ask for a value rating sheet from your accountant.) Be sure to get a receipt for the donation, though, so that you will be able to substantiate the charitable deduction on your taxes.

Archive It

We were helping a client named Audrey edit her wardrobe when we spotted a pair of ratty-looking slippers taking up space in her closet. Of course we had to ask her if she ever wore them.

"Never," Audrey answered. "They're too worn." So why on earth she was holding on to them?

Audrey explained that these were the slippers she had worn in the hospital walking the hall for hours when in labor for her first child and only daughter.

"I just *couldn't* part with them," she said.

This is what we call an "archive" item.

Archiving is reserved for "no" items that you can't part with for sentimental or nostalgic reasons. It is a way to let items go that you will never wear again but still keep them in your life because of their sentimental value. Another example might be the sweater you wore when you met the love of your life. Although years have passed, the sweater looks its age, and no longer belongs in your active wardrobe, it is an "archive" sweater.

Or maybe the item is your wedding dress—a signature piece of fashion in your life that you won't wear again, but which could have value down the road to a daughter or granddaughter who may want to wear it when she gets married. That too is an "archive" dress.

Don't confuse archiving with hoarding. In both cases, you may not want to let go of the item, but when you hoard it is not because the item has sentimental value; it is because you are being a pack rat. Face this squarely and move on. Be realistic, and approach archiving in a cut-and-dried manner so that it won't become a dumping ground for *everything*. Clothes should be archived only when they conform to one or more of the following "archive" criteria:

➤ It has sentimental value.
➤ It is a collectible.
➤ It is something your children or grandchildren might enjoy having someday.
➤ It is something you could wear to a Halloween or theme party (but remember, unless you are a stage actress, you do not need a closet full of potential costumes).

Archived clothing and accessories should be stored somewhere in your home or apartment other than your main closet. They are not part of your active wardrobe and will only get in your way. Of course, if you have a large walk-in closet with loads of space, you can put archived items in canvas garment bags and store them in the back of the closet for convenience. But the best spot to store archives is in a guest-room closet, the basement, or someplace else where they can be accessed easily whenever you need a stroll down memory lane.

One client of ours stores her archives in her attic, where she has them grouped in boxes according to their criteria for being archives—one group for sentimental items, another for collectibles, and so forth. This is a viable arrangement. It is clear to her why she is holding on to these items in the first place, allows her to easily add to the boxes whenever she reedits her wardrobe, and earmarks what these items are for, if necessary.

Demote It

Demoted garments are those you still love, are still flattering, and are appropriate to the image you want to present, but are no longer fresh. Accordingly, the statement they make isn't fresh, either. But perhaps you can still get some wear out of them if you put them to a different use.

Let's say you have an older, expensive cashmere sweater you wore for very special occasions, but it has seen better days. You gave it a "yes" to all three wardrobe clarification questions; you are not ready to leave it because it is still wearable, and you are absolutely right. Clean it up, maybe use a sweater shaver on it, and you can wear it while running errands, walking the dog, or doing chores around the house, instead of the baggy sweatshirt that makes you look and feel schlumpy. This is called "demoting" your clothes.

To demote an item is to give it a different role so that you get more wear out of it before the time arrives either to toss it or to archive it. These garments still have some life in them, and you can continue to have some fun with them. You will feel better for not wasting a usable article of clothing.

Since demoted items are still active, they too should go back into your closet on matching hangers or on shelves along with the rest of your wardrobe—but maybe in a different category. For example, instead of hanging the demoted tank top with your new ones, fold it up and place it in the workout drawer. This will eliminate confusion when getting dressed.

How to Stay Focused and Motivated

Becoming overwhelmed and feeling discouraged are the two biggest hurdles you will face during the editing step, because it is here, in the process of clarifying your wardrobe, that you are beginning the physical reshaping of your closet, and tangibly letting go of the past.

Here are some tips and strategies for beating back the blues if you find yourself becoming discouraged along the way:

▶ *Review Your Style Statement.* In the last chapter we recommended that you keep this declaration of your personal style where you will be able to see it at critical times—like now—and be inspired by it. If you feel yourself losing steam and feeling that having a root canal might be preferable right about now, review your style statement. Read it aloud. It is your personal pep talk. This will help keep you focused on the reasons you are editing your wardrobe—and help you reach your goal.

▶ *Play Music.* Put on a favorite CD, one that inspires you—consider it your "big comeback" theme music. It is important for you to establish a workable atmosphere as you try on your clothes and edit your wardrobe. Select music that keeps you going. Light a candle when you begin and blow it out when you finish. This can create a "Zen-like" zone that will keep you calm and focused.

▶ *Tidy Up as You Go.* We highly recommend that you do this, especially if you have a big closet with lots of clothes, so that you will be able to view the progress you are making. Seeing progress as you go will hearten you—a prime motivator in getting to the finish line. We recognize, however, that the more motivated you are, the less likely you will want to pause to tidy up; when you are on a roll you will want to keep going and going. This puts you in danger of suddenly finding yourself overwhelmed or exhausted by the chaos

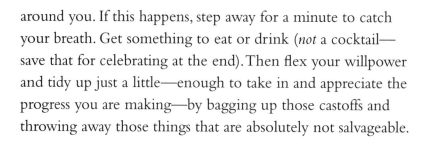

around you. If this happens, step away for a minute to catch your breath. Get something to eat or drink (*not* a cocktail—save that for celebrating at the end). Then flex your willpower and tidy up just a little—enough to take in and appreciate the progress you are making—by bagging up those castoffs and throwing away those things that are absolutely not salvageable.

➤ *Break for Lunch*. If you start the editing process first thing in the morning and work steadily, by noon you will likely have reached the midpoint. This can be a precarious time. You may be so excited by your progress that you want to keep on going—in which case you may be in danger of depleting your strength, slowing down, getting stuck, not keeping to your schedule, and even giving up. Take a break for lunch. As you return to the project with your blood sugar restored, you will look at what you have already accomplished in only a few hours, and be able to appreciate your progress all the more. You will feel your batteries recharging as you see the light at the end of the tunnel.

➤ *Edit with a Friend*. Some people are self-starters. They can set their own pace and make decisions quickly. Others have difficulty stepping outside themselves, and viewing themselves in a realistic way. This can render them vulnerable to indecision, to too-slow progress, and to giving up. If this scenario sounds like you, you might benefit from asking a friend or a relative to work with you on your wardrobe edit. An objective second opinion can be valuable in keeping you on track and moving steadily toward your destination, which is, after all, victory over your closet. A friend or relative can be a sounding board as well as a cheerleader, and help add fun to the project. Just be sure the friend or relative is someone who understands you well, whose taste and style you admire, who is trustworthy and open-minded, who can critique you without being judgmental and hurtful, and whose opinion you respect. Be warned; they may ask you to return the favor!

There, that wasn't too bad, was it? Can you recall the sense of dread you used to experience when opening your closet, and feel it slipping away into the dim, distant past? Is a sense of excitement taking its place? Many of our clients tell us that this is how they feel at this point.

Symptom: Meet Sylvia, age thirty-two and a new mom, on summer break from her career as a high school guidance counselor. At the start of her editing project, her closet was stuffed top to bottom and end to end with pre-pregnancy clothes, maternity clothes, and post-pregnancy items, all piled and/or mixed together. Some of her clothes were even stored on the floor in baskets, and she longer knew what was inside which. It was virtually impossible for her to get *into* her closet let alone get ready each day without becoming hopelessly frustrated. The mess made her feel confused, indecisive, and out of control.

Prescription: After going through the editing process, trying on each item and asking herself the three Qs, she found that she had weeded out almost 60 percent of what was in there. Of the 40 percent she kept (her active wardrobe), most she was able to put on hangers (organized by skirts, tops, jackets, pants, and evening wear) because the inventory was now much more compact and manageable. The rest she was able to store neatly in piles on a few shelves.

Outcome: There was nothing on the floor now to block access to her closet or its flow (a cluttered floor is *very bad* feng shui). Sylvia had conquered the mess, having at last achieved total clarity as to what worked, what didn't, and what was missing. How did she feel at this stage of the process?

"For one thing," she said, "I felt good about donating things to charity that weren't me anymore, or giving them away to friends, rather than just throwing them away, which would have been such a waste. But most of all, it was such a great feeling to walk into my closet, look at my wardrobe, and be able to say, 'I *love* everything in it,' instead of hating what I couldn't even see!"

Here's another story:

Symptom: Kathryn is a forty-eight-year-old married philanthropist with a grown daughter who no longer lives at home. Kathryn's house in Bloomfield Hills, Michigan, has lots of closets, all of which are hers, except one, which she generously shared with her husband Paul. Kathryn is a Chic/Avant-garde with too many unique pieces in her overgrown wardrobe, from tailored evening wear to pantsuits (in a slew of fabrics and cuts), lacy tops to camisoles. Everything was calm on the home front until Kathryn's clothes began spilling over into Paul's sole closet.

Kathryn knew something had to be done, but thought that all of her clothing was too special to part with.

Prescription: Kathryn needed to edit. She was attached to her clothing and liked the idea of having it around, but there was no room for anything new. After going through every closet, she found that in the last two years, she hadn't even worn three quarters of what she owned. She realized she had held on to items in many different sizes because her weight had fluctuated during menopause, and keeping them made her feel safe and comfortable. As a result, most of what she owned was dated and not fresh.

Kathryn

Chic - Avant - Garde

Outcome: After a major edit, which resulted in Kathryn's donating more than six large garbage bags of clothes to charity, she now contains her active wardrobe in one master closet, with one other closet used for archived items. "It's as if a humongous burden has been lifted off my back," she says. "I actually feel physically lighter." And Paul has his own closet back.

It's now time to reward yourself for all the hard work you've put in: clarifying your wardrobe, bagging the discards, organizing your closet, archiving, dropping off donations, and cleaning up. It's time to go shopping!

You are ready to move on to Step #3, where you will identify the items you need to fill in the gaps in your wardrobe. You're going to have fun finding those totally "you" garments to round out your wardrobe. Approach the stores with a list and stay on track. This will be your first test in becoming a responsible shopper.

Visual Therapy: Making the world a more beautiful place, one closet at a time.

Fill in the Gaps

Cake and Frosting

At this point in the Visual Therapy process you have a clear picture of your identity and your image. You have gone through your closet and edited out the impulse buys, the outdated trends, and the other inappropriate items that have created clutter and confusion. You have put back all your "keepers" in a well-organized, visually pleasing manner that allows for much easier access than ever before.

There, in that clean closet, is your active wardrobe. Everything in it looks great on you, and is totally appropriate for you. Now it is time to add the pieces to fill in the gaps left by your wardrobe edit.

Don't fret if your closet looks barren. The reality is that this is all that you *should* be wearing.

The bottom line is, you either feel it or you don't. If you are not comfortable and confident with what you are wearing, it will affect how you move through the day.

Less is more. Better to have less and love more than to have more and love less.

Before you can build a house, you need a solid foundation. It is the same with your wardrobe. You need reliable basics—the cake—upon which to construct your desired look. That means beginning with flattering pieces in neutral colors—black, chocolate, navy, and charcoal—and a pair of modern jeans in the style most flattering to you. To this, you will apply the frosting—the key pieces that express your defined style and complete your look.

Without the cake to support the frosting, you will find it either difficult to pull together a coherent outfit, or you will appear too busy, too over-the-top. When that happens, the focus is on your outfit, not you.

Shopping Tip

Focus on the basics first. If you must have a signature bag, belt, or shoe that will not be in stores for long because it is trendy, don't wait for it to go on sale. When it does go on sale, the trend is already on its way out.

Symptom: Jean, a forty-six-year-old brunette, is the owner of a trendy restaurant in Miami. At 5'7" and a size 4, she looks good in everything. Before Visual Therapy, her style was entirely Whimsical. She loved making a fashion statement with trendy pieces. Her fashion philosophy was "more is more." As a result, she was getting too lost in sparkle and glitz. Her outfits were full of rhinestones, prints, and textures; but lately she'd started to feel that her look was no longer age appropriate. Favorite pieces included a silver sequin capelet; jackets with floral prints; pants with paisley and animal prints like those by Cavalli; tank tops with rhinestones; loafers and strappy heels in bright colors and embellished with jewels, studs, fruit, or flowers. She owned not one white shirt and no plain anything!

Jean rightly felt she needed to tone down her look and make it less flashy. It was becoming harder and harder for her to pull together outfits that felt authentically "her" and in which she felt comfortable. After she edited her wardrobe, she realized why this was so: She had too much frosting in her wardrobe and not enough cake—those basic, monochromatic yet flattering pieces that would give her the sophisticated look she desired.

Prescription: Inspired by Visual Therapy, Jean bought some clean, ribbed solid tanks: one white, two black, and three in her favorite colors; Theory pants in black, khaki, and white; updated, sexy jeans in a plain wash and *not* trendy; sexy booties (ankle boots usually worn with jeans) in black and brown; a strappy metallic heel that goes with everything; and a couple of plain silk-cashmere blend ribbed pullover sweaters in black and brown.

By adding to her wardrobe the missing ingredient—the modern, more basic pieces in solid colors and with clean lines—she achieved an updated, refined version of her personal style, which is now a combination of Whimsical and Chic. (Adding Chic to any proclaimed style automatically sharpens the look.)

Jean

Whimsical-chic

P.T.

Outcome: Today, Jean's silhouette is no longer dominated by glitz but spiced up by those discreet touches of sparkle she loves so much and that really are her. She hasn't lost the Vegas showgirl inside her, but she now feels tastefully sexy and completely age appropriate, the exact fashion statement she wants to make.

Dos and Don'ts

Don't be consumed by the latest trends while filling your gaps. Do touch on them, choose with care, and your selection will stay modern. Some trends are so in that they are already out.

In this chapter you will create a plan of action to fill in the gaps so that when you shop you will remain focused on your mission and not be distracted by inappropriate impulse buys. When you resist being influenced or distracted by overly ambitious salespeople or friends, you can avoid being overwhelmed by the sheer abundance of clothes available to capture your eye and dazzle you. Concentrating on your priorities, you can complete your shopping mission confident that the clothing choices you make will be the right ones for you.

Clothing looks better when it skims the body. Beware of the "sausaged-in look." When shopping, always strive for a flattering silhouette.

Functional Fashion

As we are all on the go most of the time, and everyday life can sometimes be a battlefield (or at least feel like one), it is important for clothes and accessories to be fully functional as well as look great. That way, they provide added value.

Here are some examples of *functional fashion*:

➤ Stretch fabrics—the freedom of movement they allow is a life-saver, especially for travel, but soft and comfortable enough for everyday use as well.

➤ Reversible weatherproof coat—water-repellent on one side for rainy days and an attractive lightweight fabric on the other for sunny days, with pockets on both sides, so that the coat works, rain or shine.

➤ A bag (or tote) with compartments—for easy access to everything you need to have on hand, including your cell phone, business cards, wallet, tissues, keys, and much more.

Symptom: Melissa, thirty-nine years old and single, is a sales executive in the beauty supply business and lives in Tucson. Her region includes the entire West Coast. With its varying climates, temperatures along her weekly route—with no stops at home in between—can range from 50 degrees and raining to sunny and 90 degrees, so packing the right clothes for these extremes had always been a pain. In addition to putting together a week's worth of clothes to take with her, she had to lug around a suitcase full of products as well. To lighten her load and have all the clothes she required, Melissa's wardrobe and accessories had to be functional as well as good-looking.

Prescription: Melissa needed transitional-weight fabrics and layering for different temperatures. Key pieces in her new, functional wardrobe included: a medium- to lightweight reversible raincoat; a jacket with lots of pockets; a wrap and a few knits; a tote/briefcase that could accomodate files and forms, her BlackBerry, a laptop, zippered compartments for her wallet, and an outside pocket for boarding passes and identification.

Outcome: Whether she's in Seattle, San Francisco, Los Angeles, or San Diego, confident and in-control Melissa has what she needs now, and knows where everything is.

Your "Capsule" Wardrobe

Before heading off to your favorite clothing store to fill in the gaps, you need to know where you stand in terms of your foundation or "capsule" wardrobe.

"What's that?" you ask.

The following list summarizes the essential elements for a foundation wardrobe. They are the same for each personal style; the differences will be in the design of the pieces. We recommend that your

Capsule Wardrobe

capsule consist of the following neutral colors, depending on your skin tone: black, chocolate-brown, navy, charcoal, taupe, ivory, or cream. Your capsule should include:

- ➤ one dress
- ➤ one three-piece suit (jacket, pants, and skirt)
- ➤ basic and/or colored (pastels or bold) knit tops with varying necklines (V-neck, turtleneck, boat-neck, etc.) and in varying sleeve lengths (long, short, or three-quarter-length), whichever is the most flattering for you
- ➤ a white, collared shirt
- ➤ a pump, bootie, strappy heel, and flat shoe
- ➤ a pair of modern jeans
- ➤ one "frosting" jacket (tweed, suede, leather, etc.) that goes well with all of the above
- ➤ a bag or tote in basic color or with a neutral motif (such as Louis Vuitton)

These items are the bare bones, a starting point. That's why we call it a capsule wardrobe. Each part is adaptable to any style. From season to season, you will add pieces that complement your individual style and work with your foundation. This may not seem like a lot of clothes, but in fact it's more than enough because everything relates to everything else, whether the style is casual, business, or dressy.

You can build other capsule wardrobes based on this formula in other neutral colors. This will enable you to mix and match between your various capsules to create many coordinated looks. But always remember: Have less and love more.

As Coco Chanel observed, "All one needs are two or three suits as long as they—and everything to go with them—are perfect." This formula will work for everyone, with only slight adjustments in fabric weight and color, depending on the climate of the region you live in, and taking into account your individual body type (straight, curvy, or full) and defined style. Bear in mind, also, that in some areas of the country, women dress more casually than in others, in which case a three-piece suit can be replaced by a skirt and top outfit.

The exception to the rule are those people who are trendsetters or designers, people whose goal is to constantly push the envelope in what they wear because that is their career or their personal style. Unlike these people, however, you don't need to reinvent the wheel each season. If you succumb to every trend instead of becoming a savvy shopper, you defeat the purpose of identifying your perfect style. Use publications such as *Elle, Harper's Bazaar, InStyle, Lucky,* O magazine, *Vogue,* or *W* as resources and tools for inspiration.

To help you create your foundations or capsules based on your identified style, we offer several examples. Do not feel that the designer mentioned is the only one to look for when you shop. You should keep in mind the spirit of the collection that designer represents. Our recommendation is to avoid dressing head to toe in one designer's clothes. This will inhibit your originality. Many designers represent each style category—you can mix and match among them. For that purpose, we have provided after each of the following examples a checklist of other designers whose clothes represent that spirit.

Classic

Brooks Brothers is a great example of the Classic style. The shoulders and lapels of their jackets are clean and easy, rarely changing. The pant leg is straight with no flair, and hits at the waist. The skirt is typically straight with little or no detail, and the dress is as clean-lined as possible.

Other Classics include Agnona, Akris, Anne Klein, Ann Taylor,

Burberry, Gap, Tommy Hilfiger, J.Crew, Kiton, Luciano Barbera, Liz Claiborne, Loro Piana, Ralph Lauren, and Talbots.

Chic

Gucci is a great example of a collection specializing in Chic. Shoulders and lapels are sharp on the jacket, which is more fitted in the waist. Pants are slightly lower in the rise and have a little flair at the bottom of the leg. Skirts are more "pencil-like," or tapered. Dresses have a little more detail and are always sexy.

Other Chics include Armani, Banana Republic, Hugo Boss, Chanel, Club Monaco, Kenneth Cole, Express, Gucci, H&M (Chic/Bohemian), INC, Calvin Klein, Donna Karan, Laundry, Max Mara, Narciso Rodriguez, Elie Tahari, Valentino, and Zara.

Whimsical

Etro is a perfect example of Whimsical; the styles are typically more colorful and playful in nature. A jacket might have a paisley print or a brightly colored lining. Blouses sometimes have a romantic air. Pants usually have color, detail, or are a print; and skirt shapes can be retro, tulip, or full.

Other Whimsicals include Benetton, French Connection, Marc Jacobs, Betsey Johnson, Nanette Lepore, Moschino, Zac Posen, Prada, Lilly Pulitzer (Classic/Whimsical), and Louis Vuitton.

Bohemian

Chloé is a perfect example of Bohemian—feminine, hippie, and cool, less sleek-looking. On the runway the collection is mixed and matched—no hard-core hysterics that can be typecast to fashion—and looks effortless, easy, and cool.

Other Bohemians include Abercrombie & Fitch, Anna Sui, Anthropologie, Roberto Cavalli, Dolce & Gabbana, Eskandar, Matthew Williamson, Miu Miu, and Urban Outfitters.

Avant-garde

The Japanese designer Yohji Yamamoto is an excellent example of Avant-garde. Typically black, the details are usually extreme and always make a statement. Shapes are often considered "architectural" and borderline wearable art. A jacket can be deconstructed or have little or no shape. The pant can be high-waisted and wide, and a skirt could have an unusual shape, or interesting stitching or unfinished hem. Avant-garde on a budget may incorporate vintage or "doctoring-up" your own clothes.

Other Avant-gardes include Balenciaga, Comme des Garçons, Costume National, John Galliano, Jean Paul Gaultier, Lanvin, Alexander McQueen, Proenza Schouler, Top Shop, Victor & Rolf, and Issey Miyake.

Never hesitate to ask for assistance. It's okay to depend on someone else's eye to help you if you can't decide how well something fits. Take the time to try on various silhouettes and shapes to see which items looks best on your figure.

Age Appropriateness

In your twenties, anything goes. These are the years defined by trial and error, searching and education, when you enjoy complete fashion freedom. It's a time when women find themselves through the process of fashion experimentation.

In your thirties, you are coming into your own as a woman, psychologically and stylistically.

In your forties, many women experience a change in perspective, as well as physical changes. Generally it's a time to reflect and reevaluate, a time to take things to the next level.

In your fifties, most women feel they've reached a milestone, and aren't as willing to wear those stilettos anymore. Nowadays, the face (and look) of fifty is tastefully sexy—subtle, elegant, assured, and self-possessed.

Your sixties and seventies mark a period of further discovery and exploration, and are a time to focus on things you may have always wanted to do but never took the time for (hobbies, traveling), as well as spending time with family.

As you age and your priorities change, so, too, should your daily uniform. There is no cut-and-dried answer to how each individual should look to be age appropriate. As you mature, however, so should your wardrobe. Every five years, reevaluate your style and consider whether its evolution coincides with where you are in life. As a general rule, if you are a Whimsical, a Bohemian, or an Avant-garde, temper your defined style with a bit of Chic or Classic as you age and you really can't go wrong.

Six Secrets of Proactive Shopping

At this point, you have completed several steps in our process. You have edited your wardrobe. You have determined your style and identified your basic silhouette. You have a bare-bones breakdown of pieces that form your foundation or capsule wardrobe. Now you are ready to head to the store and start filling the gaps, right?

Not quite. Here are some other key shopping secrets and strategies you should know about to help facilitate this process.

Shopping proactively means shopping with a clear plan of attack for filling the voids in your wardrobe before a fashion emergency arises. Thanks to your editing, you know exactly which pieces you need to purchase and you've made a list of them.

We believe that everyone, no matter what their defined style, should have that "little black dress" in their wardrobe because it gives them a starting point, a foundation that works on many different occasions. If you have been a proactive shopper, you already have that great dress that makes you feel like a star hanging in your closet. If not, you need to find one.

A knee-length dress with a basic neckline (such as a scoop) in any fabric is simple enough that it looks great on everyone. Here are some other perfect dresses for every body type:

> ➤ **Curvy:** Emphasize your waist by buying a dress that either has a seam or gathers at the waist, is ruched or nips at that point. Go with a simple bottom, and keep all the details up top.
> ➤ **Straight (and tall):** Go for something asymmetrical in satin or jersey and longer in length to flatter your tall, lean frame. Or, consider a deep V-neck, which would look divine.
> ➤ **Straight (and short):** Shorter-length dresses will give the illusion of being taller, so skip the three-quarter-length and go for the knee.

► **Full:** Highlight your best assets, but go for something with a bit more coverage, like a scoop-neck dress with three-quarter-length sleeves and a straight body. Vertical seams and darts can sometimes create a longer, leaner look.

Shopping Tip

Buy essentials at the beginning of the season. Make indulgent purchases only when they are on sale at the end of the season. If they are sold out, perhaps it wasn't meant to be.

The key to proactive shopping is to be able to anticipate your wardrobe needs. This is done by objectively visualizing your lifestyle and preparing ahead of time for those occasions, events, or environments for which you will require different outfits. By doing this, you'll be prepared for every opportunity or invitation that comes your way. Don't miss the party because you have nothing to wear!

Create a Shopping List

People encounter a major pitfall when shopping for clothes (or anything else for that matter). They lose focus—or lack focus to begin with. Your focus is your shopping list of fill-ins, the garments that are essential to complete your active wardrobe. If you do not shop with a list of your needs—*and stick to your list*—you are more likely to buy un-related items that do not correlate with your edited wardrobe.

Your list of fill-ins enables you to ignore or disregard what is irrelevant, so that you don't waste time, energy, and money over debating whether "to buy or not to buy" something you don't need. Don't be seduced by a sale sign. If an item happens to be on sale, that's an added bonus—but it should be on your list to begin with!

Just Wondering . . .

How should I dress when shopping? Dress in your style—the image you want to present. This gives a salesperson an insight into which items might appeal to you, and saves you a lot of time.

Haste Makes Waste

It is important to fill in the gaps as soon as possible after completing your wardrobe edit. Do it while your energy level is high and all the knowledge you've gained about yourself and your wardrobe is fresh in your mind. Depending upon how great the disconnect between your image and identity (which you uncovered in Step #1), you may have either a short shopping list of fill-ins or a lengthy one that could require more time (and money) to complete. In the latter case, it is essential that you do the best you can to complete your list as quickly as your budget allows. In either case, however, it is absolutely critical not to settle for something simply to meet an arbitrary deadline or any budget requirement. You are completing your active wardrobe and if something doesn't feel right when you consider a particular item (i.e., it's not passing the three Qs), then that item is *not right for you*—no matter what the price may be, or how much time you have to shop.

If you put off filling in the gaps until you feel you have enough in your budget to cover everything on your list at once—or if you rush the process just to get it done—you may start thinking, "Time is short, the occasion is almost here, I need the item now!" As a result, you fall into the trap of shopping *reactively*. This usually spells disaster because you wind up buying something that isn't perfect but will "serve the purpose." It will probably cost you more than it should and end up hanging in your closet as soon as the occasion for which you bought it has passed. Remember the three Qs and avoid this trap!

Joy is a forty-one-year-old married math teacher who tutors during much of her free time. Her declared style is Classic/Chic. After finishing her wardrobe edit, a cocktail dress was among her fill-ins. Because it was one of the pricier items on her fill-in list, she put off looking for it. Suddenly, there was a school district event for which she needed a cocktail dress but she still hadn't gotten around to finding one. The very day of the event, she shopped frantically with a friend

who, along with the salesperson, influenced her into buying an over-priced soft lilac silk cocktail dress that hit about six inches above the knee. As Joy is on the tall side, this only enhanced the shortness of the dress, making it look way too short, not age appropriate, and the wrong attire for such a professional event. When Joy got home and reviewed her Visual Therapy guidelines and realized the costly (and embarrassing) mistake she had made, she immediately took the dress back to the store. She tried on several other dresses, this time asking herself the three Qs, and found one she loved that was appropriate in every respect.

You could make the same costly mistake of settling for something wrong if you move too quickly to fill in the gaps. In another example, Jackie, a sporty bohemian gal who rides horses and loves the outdoors, had a jacket to be worn for work on her list of fill-ins. She hurried out to get one and came across a pale yellow, fitted riding jacket that seemed perfect for her casual, mainly outdoors lifestyle. She tried it on, and gave it the three Qs. The jacket got a yes to the first Q—she did love it. And it got a yes to the third Q—it did project the right image. But in her haste she ignored the second Q (*Is it flattering?*) and in doing so failed to notice that the yellow color of the jacket completely washed her out. The answer to the second question was a resounding no, but because she was in a hurry, she bought it anyway, and regretted it later.

Don't end up like Joy and Jackie, putting yourself in a position where you are prone to making costly wrong decisions by rushing to fill in the gaps.

Just Wondering . . .

Is there a best time to shop for fill-ins? We recommend that you shop for key frosting and basic cake pieces for your wardrobe in September and April. Extra frosting pieces, which may be a bit pricey, are best purchased on sale—after Thanksgiving through January, and July through August. Mondays or Tuesdays are the best days to shop because traffic is slower, stores are less crowded and hectic, and it is much easier to shop at your own pace. To avoid feeling rushed, or having to fight your way through crowds, shop early in the week and early in the day.

Shop the Value Equation

Price isn't everything. When filling in gaps to your wardrobe, value shopping is essential, no matter what your financial situation. David Bach, author of *Start Late, Finish Rich*, says, "If you are spending more than twenty percent of your after-tax income on clothes, you are out of control. Ask yourself, 'How many hours of work will it take to pay for that?' Is it worth it?" Our very simple concept on the subject boils down to this: *Invest the most in those pieces that will give you the most wear.*

What makes an item of clothing either too pricey or a steal is its price versus its wearability. This is Visual Therapy's "value equation," and the formula works this way:

THE VALUE EQUATION

A $10 top you may wear once = $10 per wear.

A $100 top that you may wear twenty times = $5 per wear:
a much better value.

That's all there is to it. Shopping the value equation gives you a higher return on your investment, plus a great feeling of satisfaction in knowing that your clothing allowance is well spent. When, in the end you demote the garment, then finally retire or archive it, you will be able to say that whatever it may have cost you, the garment truly owed you nothing.

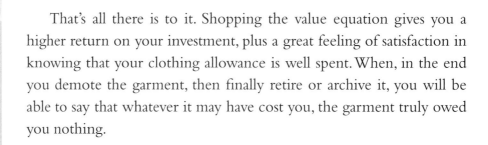

$\mathcal{P}$ut your money into clothes you are going to get a lot of wear from.

Multitask for Life

A multitasking article of clothing is an item that you will be able to use for several different purposes. For example, one of the items on the fill-in list of Catherine, age thirty-three, was a blazer. Catherine's a Bohemian/Chic with a straight (and tall) body type. Tired of her existing work/casual jackets for fall, she wanted an updated step-up jacket for casual wear that she could also wear at her job as an administrative assistant. She found a chocolate-brown suede one at Banana Republic that she absolutely loved (it passed all three Qs). It was a structured waist-length jacket with two flap pockets in front, and had cute gatherings at the shoulder that gave it a feminine, slightly romantic flair and offered a great deal of functionality—more, in fact, than she initially realized. When she wears it over monochromatic, coordinated separates, she has a suit. If she pairs it with jeans, a turtleneck, a scarf, or maybe a pair of gloves, it functions as outerwear for a great weekend or date-night look. Great jackets or blazers in leather, suede, cashmere, and wool make perfect multitasking purchases.

With multitasking purchases, you get the greatest return. Multi-tasking is extremely beneficial when traveling because you are able to pack less and still have many different outfits (for more on this, see Step #5). This strategy dovetails nicely with the value equation since an item's versatility—that is, its ability to multitask successfully with other items in your wardrobe—is an equally important consideration in shopping proactively.

So, the next time you stumble upon a unique, eye-popping piece that is definitely you, but has an eye-popping price tag to match, take into account the versatility of the item in deciding whether to purchase or to pass. Think about all the possible ways you can mix and match it within your wardrobe. If it meets the multitasking criterion, it may well be worth the money. For example, that beautiful embroidered coat may be a bit pricey, but when you think about it, you can wear it over different monochromatic separates for daytime, a dress for nighttime, and over jeans for a look that's fun, funky, and festive.

If you really love something, you will find ways to use it, and as long as it passed the other two Qs, the outfits you will create with it will be winners.

Shopping Tip

If you love bright colors but are looking for a longer, lean look, try keeping your foundation pieces (cake) dark and concentrate your color in your accessories (frosting).

Shop Realistically and with Clarity

The objective behind filling in the gaps is to complete your wardrobe so that you will be able to put all pieces into action successfully. To accomplish this, you must shop realistically: Keep your lifestyle and body type in mind as you try on each article of clothing and give them the three Qs test.

When shopping realistically, you will find it easier to avoid falling into the trap of becoming a fashion victim. You will recognize which skirts and skimpy tops are so *in* this summer but are not age appropriate for you. And you will avoid the pitfall of buying something a size too small with the intention of fitting into it after you've lost weight. Maybe you will lose that weight, and if so, good for you. But the time to go for that smaller size is later. Shopping realistically is all about *now*.

If an item does not look good on you in the store, it won't look good on you at home or anywhere else.

After flipping through her style file to help her get the "feeling" she was going for (some clippings used for inspiration can be taken literally—"I want *that* top"—while others may reflect only the spirit of the look, or the mood, you are after), Marcie was very excited about the new season. She was really into the latest trends: Prada's pleated print skirts, embellished twinsets, round-toe shoes, and exotic animal-print bags. She called a salesperson she knew at her favorite clothing

Marcie

store in Cincinnati to give her notice that she would be coming in (a subject we will get to shortly), and described the looks she liked and sought to emulate, even giving the salesperson the page numbers of the magazines from which Marcie had clipped pictures.

Even though Marcie was worried about sticking to her budget, she went ahead anyway and purchased everything available in her size until she had almost maxed out her credit card. As a result, she ended up with a closet full of clothes that were very "this season."

Marcie is predominantly a Classic, with a hint of Whimiscal. But here's the catch: She works as an executive assistant in a conservative firm where she can't wear most of what she bought because it would be inappropriate. As such, she made a very costly mistake. She can't fully utilize her wardrobe now, and it will be dated in the very near future. She should have spent the majority of her money on a foundation of clean Classic items and indulged her trendy Whimsical side more in accessories.

Be consistent: Your defined style should work wherever you are, whatever the occasion—city or country, dressy or casual. Be consistent: Figure out what it is that excites you fashion-wise and let your wardrobe and style work for you fully.

Shopping with clarity means sticking to your defined style no matter what temptations arise, and staying on target. Shop from your list and ask the three Qs about each item, thereby ensuring that everything you buy works with your wardrobe, is worth the money you are spending on it, and that you make no mistakes. Shopping with clarity means that you will be able to pass up the sale items you really don't need, and the trendy ones that may not really be you. That way, there will be no regrets in your closet.

Have the store's fitter or tailor (if available) give you a thorough going-over when you try on a garment. If no one is present to help you, be sure to walk around, sit down, and bend over to ensure comfort and a proper fit. Ask yourself: Can I drive comfortably in this? Can I raise my arms? Can I dance in it?

Follow the same strategy with handbags and shoes. Do you prefer to carry a bag snugly under your arm, or hold it by the handles in one hand? Do you prefer soft or hard leather (that is, slouchy or tailored)? For shoes, make sure you can walk in them for more than five minutes without your feet hurting. Do your feet stay in them or do your heels slip out of the back? There is nothing worse than an uncomfortable shoe—it can ruin your day, not to mention your foot. We sometimes dub heels "stand-and-pose" or "limousine" shoes because while they may look good, they are so uncomfortable you cannot walk in them!

Your Visual Therapy Size Search Guide

Even if it says it's a European size 10, it's probably an 8. This can be frustrating. That's why we insist you try everything on. Use the following size guide as a reference tool when shopping.

WOMEN'S APPAREL*

SIZE	XXS	XS	S	M	L	XL	XXL	XXXL
JEANSWEAR [JNS]	22–23	24–25	26–27	28–29	30–31	32–33	34–35	36–38
USA	**2**	**4**	**6**	**8**	**10**	**12**	**14**	**16**
ITALY [IT]	36	38	40	42	44	46	48	50
UK	4	6	8	10	12	14	16	18
EUROPE [EU]	32	34	36	38	40	42	44	46
JAPAN [JPN]	5	7	9	11	13	15	17	19

WOMEN'S FOOTWEAR

SIZE	XXS	XS	S	M	L	XL	XXL	XXXL
USA	**5–5.5**	**6–6.5**	**7–7.5**	**8–8.5**	**9–9.5**	**10–10.5**	**11–11.5**	**12**
IT–EU	35–35.5	36–36.5	37–37.5	38–38.5	39–39.5	40–40.5	41–41.5	42–42.5
UK	2–2.5	3–3.5	4–4.5	5–5.5	6–6.5	7–7.5	8–8.5	9
JPN	22–22.5	23–23.5	24–24.5	25–25.5	26–26.5	27–27.5	28–28.5	29

WOMEN'S BELTS

SIZE	XXS	XS	S	M	L	XL	XXL	XXXL
LENGTH IN INCHES	**24"**	**26"**	**28"**	**30"**	**32"**	**34"**	**36"**	**38"**
LENGTH IN CM	60 cm	65 cm	70 cm	75 cm	80 cm	85 cm	90 cm	95 cm

*International size used mostly for jeans

Build Relationships with Salespeople

Many larger department stores offer complimentary personal shoppers as a convenience for the customers. When you build a relationship with a personal shopper, you have someone on your team who can help you with your fill-in list and who also can let you know about new items available that fit your style. Maximize your shopping experience by scheduling a time to work with your personal shopper. Discuss in advance the items on your list so your personal shopper can preselect a number of them in time for your appointment.

A personal shopper can also keep you informed about upcoming sales. With her scouting for your size and style, you can buy that extravagant piece you've been eyeing without breaking the bank.

With a personal shopper, there is never an obligation to buy; if an item doesn't work (remember, it must get a yes to all three Qs), then it doesn't work, period. On the other hand, it is bad form (as well as bad for the relationship) to ask a personal shopper to find certain items, lay them aside for you, alert you to a sale, and then for you to come into the store unannounced and buy from another salesperson, or use another salesperson on your next visit. Personal shoppers are there to build relationships with loyal customers but at the same time to sell merchandise and make money—respect that. If you are loyal to your personal shopper, your personal shopper will be loyal to you. Always observe proper shopping etiquette and telephone in advance to set up an appointment so that your trip to the store doesn't conflict with your personal shopper's day off.

It is also important to remember that all sales associates and personal shoppers have sales goals. Be sure that you communicate clearly to your salesperson your budget and needs. Where did Marcie go wrong? Marcie failed to stay focused and did a poor job of communicating her priorities. She didn't mesh her style with her lifestyle. Her shopper took her style file suggestions literally and pulled items that exceeded Marcie's budget.

Unlike outside consultants, whose fees for their services as personal shoppers will range widely, it's a well-kept secret that most stores do not charge for their in-house personal shoppers' services. If your favorite department or clothing stores do not have a personal shopping service, as an alternative you may be able to build a relationship with one of the store's sales consultants who can assist in you in a similar fashion. Use discretion when choosing a shopper. Think long-term by selecting someone you feel comfortable with, who you feel is completely trustworthy, and with whom you can communicate effectively.

Online Shopping

If you live in an area where your choice of clothing stores is severely limited and you do not mind returning things that don't fit or aren't suitable, then online or catalogue shopping may be the right tool for building your wardrobe. But make sure you know and understand the online store's return and refund policies before you buy. We believe it is important—indeed, *critical*—to be able to touch, to feel, and to try on clothing (so you can give it the three Qs) before you buy. This is all part of shopping realistically. Obviously, you cannot do that any of those things when shopping on the Internet. But if there is a store or designer you know well, and you know definitively that you are a size 6 in that store or designer's sizes, you can supplement your wardrobe by buying from them online because you know the item will be a sure fit.

The Internet is a great way to gather information, however, and many designers and stores offer Web sites that you can and should use for that purpose. Even if a designer's line may be beyond your budget, you can discover a look or spirit that may inspire you to find something similar in your style at a local store, possibly even at a lower price.

Since accessories do not come in sizes, the need to touch, to feel, and to try them on isn't as critical. Shopping for them online may be a way of expanding your shopping reach to find a unique piece that is not available in your hometown.

Remember, you have flexibility in how many gaps to fill before starting to pull your wardrobe together. It is not essential that you fill in *all* gaps at once. Do so at a pace that is comfortable, affordable, and makes sense to you. If you can't find an item to fill a particular gap now, come back to it in a week, a month, or whenever your favorite clothing store is scheduled to receive its next shipment of new items. Don't fall into the "this will do" syndrome and opt for second best just to fill a gap quickly.

Complete each of these steps to the degree required, and you can avoid common shopping mistakes. For example, you may find yourself buying clothes you already own—we call this "Repeat Purchase Syndrome"—or buying things that are wholly inappropriate to your true (rather than your perceived) personal style which we've dubbed "Delusional Purchase Syndrome." Likewise, while editing your wardrobe, you may risk getting rid of inexpensive items that are well suited to your defined style while holding on to other, more expensive, yet far less appropriate articles of clothing for the wrong reason: just because they were expensive! By following our formula, you will experience the optimal, lasting, positive results of Visual Therapy.

Once you have filled in the gaps in your wardrobe, you can really begin to "shop your closet." All you need is hanging before you.

Pull It All Together

Being Prepared, Made Easy

Now that you have filled the gaps in your edited wardrobe, you have the pieces necessary to create the different looks you will need for every occasion.

In this step, you will actually create those outfits—your "optimal looks"—and document them in picture and word for quick, easy reference. From here on in, looking and feeling fabulous will be an effortless—and fun—task.

Your wardrobe should contain old and new friends that come together to support you through life.

What You Will Need

To complete this step, you should add the following items to your Visual Therapy Wardrobe Survival Kit:

➤ *A Polaroid instant camera and film*. We recommend you use a Polaroid for this step rather than a 35mm or digital camera because the results are *immediate*. You snap the photo, press a button, and *voilà*, the printed picture (measuring 3.5" x 4.2") is there at your fingertips. You see each outfit in its entirety, and can determine whether the look is perfect as is or needs some adjustment. You can pick up a basic-model camera—the Polaroid Classic—for around $35 at any camera store, department store with a camera department, or drugstore such as Duane Reade or Walgreens. They can also be ordered online at www.polaroid.com. If you think you will be putting together a lot of outfits for documentation, you have the option of buying a three-pack of film.

➤ *Digital camera*. Althouth we prefer Polaroid pictures for their immediacy, a digital camera is also an option. Just be sure to print out the pictures and label them with a description of the look, or save them in a folder on your computer.

➤ *A photo album with picture pockets*. We recommend that you buy a photo album that measures 5" x 5" or 5" x 7" for cataloguing your outfits—we call it a "Look Book." An album can hold up to 200 three-by-five pictures, making it ideal for long-term use. You can pick up a suitable album at any Staples, OfficeMax, or well-stocked stationery or department store.

➤ *A recipe box.* This is another great option. You can file and categorize your photos in it, and add and remove them with ease.

The full-length mirror you used when editing your wardrobe (described in Step #2) is essential for this step, too; you will want to try on each outfit you pull together and see yourself in it so that you can make any needed adjustments before final documentation and cataloguing in your Look Book.

*T*hree-tenths of good appearance is due to nature, *seven-tenths to dress.* —Ancient Chinese saying

Formulating "Optimal Looks"

In order to create different outfit formulas ("optimal looks") for all occasions, you need to give some thought to what your average week is like. An outfit formula breaks down your requirements into categories that make getting dressed a simple matter. It allows you to create a fully organized system that streamlines the decision-making process in getting dressed or packing.

There are as many potential outfit formulas as there are facets of your lifestyle, but don't go overboard. You can keep creating looks endlessly, so focus on the best ones. The idea is to create only optimal looks, those you really love and feel best wearing. Think about what your principal activities are for a given week, how you want to dress on these occasions, and create outfit formulas for them accordingly. First, break down your major activities into categories like this:

- ➤ daytime-weekday
- ➤ daytime-weekend
- ➤ day-into-evening
- ➤ business casual
- ➤ business dressy
- ➤ evening/date night
- ➤ special events

Camille, a twenty-nine-year-old marketing consultant for a global consulting firm who lives in Washington, D.C., and is engaged to be married next spring, had just gotten home from shopping for her fill-ins and was so excited that she wanted to start pulling together her optimal looks right away. She invited over a friend, put on her favorite music, turned off the phone, and got to work. A Classic/Chic, she began by making her list of major activities for which she needed outfit formulas, the most important category being her business formulas for dressing at her office. She quickly realized that by using her capsules as a foundation—for example, by pairing her chocolate two-button silk blazer from Banana Republic with the matching pant and skirt—she actually has two suits in one. By swapping the pant for the skirt and changing a brown knit cotton tee for an ivory V-neck sleeveless shirt, she can easily go for a flirtier look. And by switching accessories, she could create different moods from that one small capsule.

She also bought from Banana Republic a taupe A-line knee-length suede skirt, and an army-green safari-style jacket to mix into her existing wardrobe. Both pieces she can wear day-into-evening simply by changing what is going with it. At the office she will go for a more conservative (but still great) look by pairing the suede skirt with her white collared shirt and brown pumps from last season; at night she will wear her new black leather Anne Klein knee-length boots, with a black boat neck with roll collar chiffon top, which looks *oh-so-chic.*

Having assembled different combinations from her wardrobe and fill-ins, all of them examined in her full-length mirror to decide which were optimal, Camille suddenly realized it was now midnight. She had created more than thirty-five looks for herself in her various categories, and every one of them was optimal! Camille felt confident and in control of her image for every aspect of her life.

It is within the first few seconds of meeting you that people formulate their impression; unfortunately, it may be the only one. Your style is part of the impression you make.

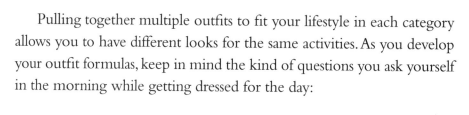

Pulling together multiple outfits to fit your lifestyle in each category allows you to have different looks for the same activities. As you develop your outfit formulas, keep in mind the kind of questions you ask yourself in the morning while getting dressed for the day:

> **"What's the weather forecast?"** If it is going to be a rainy day, you *don't* want an outfit formula that includes suede, silk, or other delicate fabrics. But you *do* want to wear shoes that can weather the storm, maybe something with a rubber sole, or a waterproof bootie made for rain or snow.

> **"Do I have any meetings scheduled?"** What you should wear depends on who, what, and where you are meeting. For example, if you have an important business meeting you want an outfit formula that will help determine how you want that group to perceive you (that is, approachable, smart, cute, sexy, powerful). That look will vary depending upon who you are meeting with—a church group, your accountant or attorney, or a friend for lunch. Think of the environment (office, store, etc.) and the "role" you will play (client, employee, or boss), as well as whatever expectations others may have of you. When putting together different formulas, be they formal, casual, or fun you always want to look the part to be the most effective throughout your day.

> **"Will I be going out tonight?"** If you are going to be ending your day at a new local hot spot, you don't want the same look you wore to work or while running errands during the day. Undoubtedly there will be occasions when you won't have time to go home and change; a day-to-evening formula can make that transition for you. For a day-to-evening optimal look, consider changing from your white shirt to a sexy camisole. Take your black clutch out of your tote. Remove your jacket and add a wrap.

➤ **"Will I be doing a lot of walking?"** Anticipation is key in developing formulas and accessories. For example, there may be times when you will meet a friend at a museum and be walking on hard, uncarpeted floors all afternoon. When this is the case, you will want a look that doesn't include your highest heels.

Asking questions like these now will help guide you later when pulling together outfits that will make you look and feel comfortable, appropriate, and prepared for every occasion.

Carmen is twenty-three and lives in Miami, where she recently received her degree in physical therapy and plans to quit her two part-time jobs—one as a hostess, the other as a trainer at a local gym—to pursue a career as a physical therapist. Her lifestyle at the moment is very casual. A size 6 on top and an 8 on the bottom, she generally feels sexy and confident. At night she prefers to wear black tube-top dresses and form-fitting cotton T-shirts, or tanks with Capri jeans or short denim skirts. During the day she chooses bright colors like pink, aqua, and peach, and wears sundresses with tropical prints in solid jersey or cotton. When she was a student, she had been on a pretty strict budget, but she splurges every now and again on things such as a romantic sleeveless woven black top with ruffles from Bebe, a lacy, chiffon summer dress from BCBG, or even a wedge or slide shoe.

Carmen's fashion dilemma is that she has a tendency to dress too sexy for all occasions. As a result, her entire wardrobe is on the risqué side. As she enters her new career as a physical therapist, she needs to be taken seriously and treated with respect, but still be tastefully sexy. The image she wants to project in both her casual and work life is confident, warm (but not hot), and capable.

Carmen

Sexy-chic

R.T.

Office No-Nos

NO see-through clothing.

NO sneakers. Save them for the gym, the park, or a sporty weekend look.

NO flip-flops. Even if you have a casual-dress policy at work, we have yet to see a person passed over for a promotion for looking *too* professional or *too* neat. Dress for the job you want.

NO sequins, satins, or anything over-the-top during the day, when in corporate environments. If you have the urge to "bling," remember this: You want your colleagues and clients to be dazzled by *you,* not the sparkle *on* you. A simple pair of diamond studs or pearls and a beautiful watch is sufficient for professional attire.

Putting it together the Visual Therapy way is how Carmen connected the dots and made this happen. For her new career, she purchased white gauchos that she will tame during the day with a white tank and her wedge heels. (She is able to wear most of her current wardrobe at night to bars with friends.) She also bought a few easy-fitting trousers (low-rise, fuller leg, and slightly flared at the bottom) so she still feels cute at work without wearing pants that are too tight or inappropriate. She paired these with some tanks (throwing a cardigan over her shoulders), and short-sleeve scoop-neck colored tops to give herself some color!

Ask youself: "Where am I going in this?" Imagine yourself dressed in the outfit on the occasion you intend to wear it—say, dinner and a movie. If you can't see yourself in both places in the same outfit, then it is not appropriate.

Recipe for Success

To pull together your various looks, use the same Visual Therapy recipe for style greatness you learned in Step #3: That is, *start with your basic formula*—articles of flattering clothing that you use as a base—and then dress your formula up or down with accessories, as needed.

Start monochromatic. This, your cake, can be as simple as a knit top (a ribbed tank, a V-neck shirt, a turtleneck sweater, etc.) and a pair of jeans. Then add your frosting pieces and experiment until you've assembled the outfits you really love. Always remember, you are aiming for *optimal* looks, the ones you feel fabulous in.

Be consistent. Always keep in mind your defined style (Step #1) when developing your various looks, and the results will leave you feeling comfortable and natural.

Caroline is twenty-nine, lives in Dallas, and works from home as a realtor. She has created a variety of casual looks to meet her needs. A Classic/Chic, she utilizes a white shirt or twinset with a pair of flattering khakis, loafers, or a ballerina flat as her basic weekday casual formula. She completes her look with diamond or pearl stud earrings

Caroline

Classic
Chic

R.T.

and a handbag or tote in chocolate-brown leather. She keeps her makeup fresh and natural.

To dress this formula up a little for lunch with the girls, she will wear a flirty skirt and a pair of strappy heels. She finishes the look by stepping up her accessories and turns up the volume on her hair and makeup.

Once a week, Caroline and her husband have a date night. For this occasion, she takes a fitted jacket from one of her suits and pairs it with jeans and a sexy knit top—maybe a V-neck or a form-fitting turtleneck. She tops off her look with a pair of sexy drop earrings.

This is how Caroline achieves the feminine, sexy, modern Classic/Chic look that she adores, and she does it every day.

Casual does not mean sloppy. Clothes should always be neat, clean, and coordinated.

If you need inspiration to devise your different looks, refer to the Style File we suggested you create in Step #1, or glance through more fashion magazines for good ideas. Consider asking a friend or family member with a similar personal style, and whose look you admire, to help you create your outfit formulas.

Nothing Lasts Forever

At some point, you will probably want or need to revise or update your outfit formulas. After all, our lifestyles change over time, as do our bodies and activities. Clothes wear out and must be replaced, or we grow tired of certain pieces. Seasonal changes are also necessary (for more on this, see Step #5). Therefore, you will have to adjust your formulas to revitalize them. But if you stay true to your defined style, making these adjustments can be effortless. Just don't get stuck in a time warp.

Symptom: Cindy, thirty-seven, and a full-time mother of two boys, is petite, with blond hair and tanned skin. Her wardrobe is bright and cheery, much like the weather in the part of the South where she lives. However, she has come to a stage in her life where, although she is essentially happy with what's in her closet, she is tired of being labeled "cute" and wants to add some Chic-ness to her Whimsical nature. She has the Whimsical look down pat—there is no black or neutral anything in her wardrobe, which consists mainly of cropped pants in every color, printed and embroidered T-shirts, skirt-and-top "uniforms" (tops and bottoms made of the same prints that are sold as an outfit). She migrated to clothes like that because they made it a no-brainer to get ready in the morning. That was her formula, and now she's looking for a change.

Prescription: Cindy felt ready to take her style to the next level. She pared down her favorites to a few items, and decided it was time to separate the uniforms and add in some neutral-colored Capri pants or skirts. This is a good example of wardrobe evolution! She treated herself to a pair of diamond studs, which go with everything, and bought some lightweight cardigans in brights and neutrals to go with her Capri formula or with the printed pants and skirts.

Cindy

whimsical
Chic

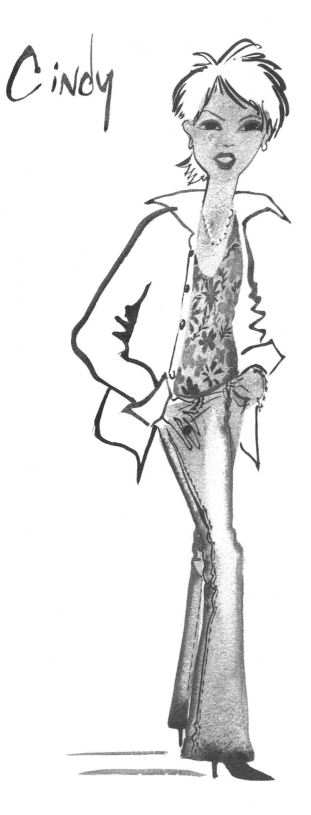

R.T.

Outcome: As cute as Cindy is (and probably always will be), people have started to notice a Chic edge to her appearance, and begun describing her look as "sleek"—just what she wanted.

TIP: Create an Inspiration Board

Fashion designers use "inspiration boards" to spark ideas for each new season. These are generally bulletin boards on which they tack images from books and magazines, setting the tone and giving direction for the upcoming season—anything that inspires them. Consider adapting the same concept for your own use. Some of our clients like to use inspiration boards in addition to their Style File for generating instant updates, making seasonal changes, and staying motivated, because they can hang them in their closet or over their desk in their den or home office where they are readily visible. Like your Style File, the focus of your inspiration board should be fashion spreads, editorials, and advertisements that depict or describe clothing, accessories, and moods that appeal to your personal style. At the same time, we also recommend tacking up photos of your kids, the family pet, a room décor you especially admire, and other things meaningful to you, to create a collage representative of the *lifestyle* to which you aspire. This exercise may strike you as being silly at first, but it will provide you with direction and focus as you start to think about the upcoming season and how you may update your wardrobe by adding certain pieces.

$\mathcal{T}$he power suit is the secret to success. A basic black, navy, or charcoal suit is essential to a strong work wardrobe.

Documenting Outfits for Fast Reference

Documenting your fully accessorized looks for each major activity category and cataloguing them in your Look Book provides you with a foolproof guide for fast, stress-free dressing and easy packing for trips (see Step #5 for some packing tips). Here's how to do it.

Document your optimal looks by taking a snapshot of yourself in each outfit, head to toe. Obviously, it will be impractical to photograph yourself in the outfit unless you are using a digital camera with a self-timer. Otherwise, having a friend or relative present to help you can come in handy in addition to being a lot of fun (even if you must promise to return the favor someday). It's best to be photographed in the look so you can see for yourself whether it fits, and whether you're really "feelin' it."

Stand before a clean, light-colored wall or door if your look is dark (or a dark-colored wall or door if your look is light) and have your friend snap a photo of you in each outfit to be documented. If you are your own photographer, we recommend that you lay each outfit, complete with shoes and accessories, on a clean, flat, well-lit surface, such as a light-colored rug, countertop or table, for your pictures. Either method, however, will get you the record you need for your Look Book.

When you have photographed each outfit formula, write the name of the major activity category the outfit belongs in (i.e., daytime-weekday) on the Polaroid or accurately label your digital photo. Then write a full description of the outfit. (Remember, don't leave out the accessories.)

Symptom: Carrie, a marketing executive for a telecommunications company, is a Chic in her thirties. Once a Bohemian, she now aimed for a more sophisticated look. She was now at this stage of the Visual Therapy process, so she called up a friend, Janet (who is also a Chic), to help her document her optimal looks. They spent an afternoon pulling together outfits for Carrie, and Janet took the Polaroid pictures.

Prescription: She started by thinking of five looks for each of her major activity categories—for business, for date night, and so on. She realized, however (and much to her dismay), that there are a lot more business days than date nights, so for the business category, she came up with twelve outfits. At the end of the session, Carrie had more than forty optimal looks from all her combinations to put in her Look Book.

Outcome: Carrie and Janet had so much fun doing this together that Janet, who had also gone through the Visual Therapy process, booked Carrie for the very next weekend to help her "pull it all together."

Just Wondering . . .

Why don't men have wardrobe problems like women? Men *do* have wardrobe problems. It is just a little easier for them because men's fashions do not change as often or as drastically as women's. Men can put on their uniform (be it a suit or an actual uniform) every day. Unlike women, they have fewer choices to make—shoes, pants, shirt, tie, etc. Men have always tended to shop for clothing with a list, and they rarely deviate from it.

The Two-Second Choice

Now that you have completed documenting your outfit formulas for a host of activities, you should feel that you have a solid wardrobe and a clearer, more confident sense of self.

Gone are the days where you found yourself standing in your closet, thinking, "I have nothing to wear!" And because you have documented your wardrobe combinations, you will no longer waste time and energy pondering over what goes best with what for which occasion. It gives you peace of mind to know that you have the perfect look for every activity. By flipping though your Look Book, dressing for any occasion is now a matter of making what we call the Visual Therapy "Two-Second Choice"—because that is how long it will take to choose what to wear. You are free at last to focus your energies not on your closet, but on more important matters.

Danielle   chic

R.T.

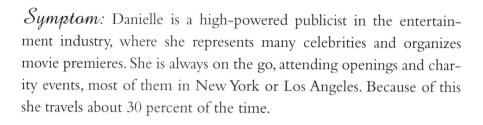

Symptom: Danielle is a high-powered publicist in the entertainment industry, where she represents many celebrities and organizes movie premieres. She is always on the go, attending openings and charity events, most of them in New York or Los Angeles. Because of this she travels about 30 percent of the time.

Prescription: She *lives* by her formulas and utilizes her Look Book to pack for trips.

Outcome: After she determines what she will be doing during a trip, she selects the appropriate outfits from among the Polaroids in her Look Book. This takes her about two seconds, and she is able to pack her suitcase in no time. For example, if she has meetings with producers all day and must go directly to a premiere at night, in the daytime she will wear a black pantsuit with a sexy underpinning (deep V-neck), along with a jacket. Later, to carry her into an evening look, she will remove the jacket, add a wrap and a pair of drop earrings and a sexier, higher, strappy shoe.

Often, she will slip the Polaroids out of her Look Book and take them with her so that she can refer to them on the road if she needs to.

The key to stress-free dressing is seeing what is in your closet and having easy access to it. A closet that's overstuffed blinds you to possibilities. Your wardrobe can't evolve because there is literally no room to grow. This translates to no room in your life for change, or for anything new to be able to enter it. That's where Step #5 comes in.

Nurture the New You

The Evolving You

Maintaining and building upon the great sense of personal style you have achieved through the previous four steps of the Visual Therapy process is the key to continuing your personal evolution. Nurturing the new you involves two essential elements:

1. Keeping your look fresh
2. Taking proper care of your wardrobe

Step #5 will show you how to accomplish both with a little effort in very little time.

Maintaining yourself and your wardrobe is a form of self-respect.

What You Will Need

You will want to have the following items on hand in your Visual Therapy Wardrobe Survival Kit for ongoing use. They can be purchased at any drugstore or discount department store.

- **Clothes brush.** To give your jackets and suits staying power by preventing dust and other elements from clogging the garment's ability to "breathe." It looks like a hairbrush with very tight bristles.
- **Lint brush** or **tape-roller.** To remove lint, dust, and other particles (such as hair) from garments to keep them looking fresh.
- **Sweater shaver.** To remove the little balls (pills) that accumulate on sweaters. It comes battery powered with a protective screen to prevent damage to your sweater. A lifesaver!
- **Shoetrees.** To prolong the life of your shoes and to prevent creases or the collapsing of the toe.
- **Instant shoeshine kit.** Great for those quick fixes, and to clean up a slightly scarred or scuffed shoe before a meeting or a date.
- **Emergency sewing kit.** Compact, easy to use and store, these kits come with an assortment of needles and different colored threads for fast emergency repairs at work or on the road. Keep one in your office drawer and one at home, so that you can quickly reattach that loose button or drooping hem. Many hotels will have one available for your use if you request it, but don't count on this; keep one in your luggage just in case. In addition to drug and department stores, kits are available at shops such as Jo-Ann Fabric and Craft that specialize in sewing supplies.
- **Hand steamer.** These are terrific little lifesavers, perfect for

spot steaming wrinkles and prolonging the life and freshness of dresses and suits. They are easy to use and take up very little space. Be careful using with silk and satins, though, where it may cause water stains.

➤ **Shout wipes.** Portable towelettes for quick removal of tough stains.

➤ **Woolite.** A mild fabric wash containing no bleach.

➤ **Febreze.** A spray that removes food and smoke odors from clothing.

Keeping Your Look Fresh

Make Instant Updates and Seasonal Changes

Instant updates can provide the little jump-start you need when your look is getting stale or you'd like to retire some pieces of your wardrobe. We all need that kind of pick-me-up once in a while. Beware of getting so caught up in the moment that you start shopping with an "I don't know what I want, but I want something new" attitude. You are likely to make some costly mistakes that way, such as buying a trendy item that doesn't fit your style. A subtle change that refreshes your look may be all you need. You never know; it may already be hanging there in your closet. You may simply need to alter a piece and adjust the fit to give it new life.

Let's say your style is Classic, and you are comfortable with your style, but also a bit bored. Instead of buying a whole new Classic wardrobe, consider changing the handbag you carry. Buy one that is well within your Classic style but sports a different detail or offers new twist. A chocolate-brown woven Bottega Veneta bag is a subtle but always modern update. Depending on your age and budget, a fun bag

or tote from the Gap in your favorite fun color, or a new red or burgundy handbag from Coach, can also do the trick. With one new accessory, you can perk up your whole look instantly.

Seasonal changes in your look also keep you up-to-date and fresh. Here are some tricks of our trade that will help:

➤ A fabulous new pair of shoes will automatically revive your entire look. They can be the final touch that can pull an outfit together. From season to season there is always a slight shape and/or heel change. Kate, a forty-something mother of two who lives in Los Angeles, admits that she is somewhat of a hippie at heart and defines her style as Bohemian/Chic. She loves sleek, laid-back, and sexy. Recently, while at a party, she glanced around the room and saw that everybody was wearing pointed toes with spiked heels while she had on a pair of round-toe wedges from last season. She thought, "I should demote this shoe to my more casual looks and check out the new shapes and styles." Let's face it, you can have a rockin' outfit on, but if your shoes are wrong, you might as well go home because that is what you will focus on all night.

➤ During the winter, a soft or textured scarf and fitted gloves in a bold color, coordinated to go with your classic overcoat, may be all you need to update your look.

➤ Infuse newness into your wardrobe by popping the new color of the season in a simple tee or tank worn under a blazer, vest, or cardigan. Wolford makes nice underpinnings. They can be worn alone, are usually knit (not a woven cotton), and are a fine foundation piece.

➤ A new handbag in your style (chosen as carefully as you would a new jacket or pair of pants) can instantly transform you.

➤ If you wear eyeglasses or sunglasses, turn them into your most important accessory (instead of your oldest) by changing the frames. After all, you wear them daily and they are the first thing people see.

➤ A heavy, dark lipstick will look out of place with light summer clothes. From dewy in spring to deeper and richer in the fall, and in finishes from shimmery to matte, beauty's beat changes in both color and consistency. Each season, a simple change of color in lipstick or eye shadow can make a difference.

TIP: *Revisit Your Style File and Inspiration Board*

The evolution of your style is part of keeping it fresh. Revisit the clippings in your Style File (see Step #1) and on your inspiration board (see Step #4) to inspire and give you direction with your update. Keep them both fresh each season by perusing issues of fashion and/or lifestyle magazines for new looks or separates that catch your eye. You might see a new haircut on a model that you particularly like, or a skirt or this season's pattern or color that will add the newness your wardrobe needs. Clip out the pages and add them to your Style File and inspiration board. Typically, these issues hit the newsstand in February/March for spring and September for fall.

Symptom: Jenn is a full-time philanthropist in her early thirties, with a heart of gold. She works with many local charities, mostly those serving to the arts. Her calendar is filled with dinner dates, parties, and benefits. She loves to dress up for every occasion, and because she attends so many, she had come to feel she had worn to death every look in her arsenal. But she didn't want to reinvent the wheel or break the

Jenn

whimsical

R.T.

bank buying a whole new wardrobe. What she needed was an instant update to help her finish out the season, and better reflect her whimsical nature.

Prescription: First, she sought inspiration from her Style File, where she immediately found several magazine clippings she had saved while doing Step #1 of Visual Therapy. They included illustrations of bold, fun accessories—necklaces, earrings, and bracelets with a 1940s retro feeling that appealed to her. Next, she went browsing in a flea market one Sunday afternoon and she came upon some wonderful, unique pieces, much like the pictures in her Style File, that were actually from the 1940s. She loved them and bought them immediately.

When Jenn got home with her newfound treasures, she put them on, examined them in the mirror, and reviewed her outfits with the new accessories. They all went well together. To finish the job, she visited her hairdresser and changed her hair color—only slightly, but it was a much needed and welcome change for her personally. Later, she went to the makeup counter at her local department store and bought a new shade of lipstick.

Outcome: Wearing one of her favorite outfits with the new accessories and her new and exciting makeup and hair, she attended a party the following week and wowed all her friends with her instant update.

Edit Your Wardrobe Seasonally

Set aside some time each season to do a wardrobe review and edit. Use this seasonal wardrobe clarification as an opportunity to keep your wardrobe under control by reviewing key pieces and asking yourself the three Qs from Step #2: "Do I love it?" "Is it flattering?" "Does it reflect my style?"

Doing a wardrobe clarification before the season changes will enable you to see immediately if any items you held onto after your last edit went unworn, or weren't worn as often as you expected. This may be a good time to demote those pieces to another category (casual wear, for example), archive them, or give them away.

When you are done with your seasonal review and edit, go shopping with your list in hand to fill in the gaps for the updated look you seek. You're set until next season. In this way, you maintain control over your closet, thus inspiring control in your life. The more streamlined your wardrobe, the more focused it will be. And the more often you continue this process, the quicker and easier it becomes.

You can't keep adding without taking things away or you will have no room to grow.

Store Off-Season Clothes

Always separate your spring clothing from your fall clothing. Keeping your off-season clothes together with your working wardrobe will only confuse you visually. It will cause you to look at—and be distracted by—pieces that are not appropriate for the current time of year.

Out of sight is best. If you have a separate closet in another part of your home, store off-season clothes there. Just make sure it is a cool, dry place. If storage space is limited and your closet is the only alternative, store off-season pieces to the back of the closet, as far away as possible from your active wardrobe. Your active wardrobe should always be up front, and in the most accessible part of your closet, period!

Here are some other helpful hints for off-season storage:

➤ Set aside items you will need for any upcoming trips or vacations in a different climate. For example, if while storing your summer clothes for winter you know you will be visiting Florida in January, keep some summer clothes on hand. This is your resort section. During summer, keep a favorite cashmere or medium-weight sweater handy for those occasionally chilly or rainy days or trips to an overly air-conditioned movie theater.

➤ Store your hanging off-season clothes in canvas garment bags with a clear plastic side so you can see what is inside. Allow fabric to breathe, if possible. Doing so will help keep your whites fresher for the summer and your wools/cashmeres fresher for the winter.

➤ Cedar blocks are also good for storing wools or cashmere garments. If storage will be long-term, mothballs or lavender work well, too. Of the three, we prefer the smell of lavender to cedar and mothballs, and you probably do, too.

➤ Archived items should also be stored in canvas or fabric bags after cleaning to protect them from moths, dust, or dirt that could settle in permanently.

Proper Care of Your Wardrobe

Since your clothes are a reflection of you, you want them to always look good. This means replacing your whites when they are no longer white and understanding when and how to launder or dry-clean your garments to prolong their life.

Here are some helpful hints for properly maintaining the investment you have made in your wardrobe.

Cleaning Suits and Dresses

➤ Lightly brush heavy wool or cashmere garments every few weeks with a clothes brush after you have worn them. This helps revitalize the fabric.

➤ In most climates, a suit can be worn at least ten times before it has to be dry-cleaned. Jackets should be cleaned half as often as your trousers. (No, the color won't change noticeably.)

➤ Press trousers and skirts after every third wearing, on average, or as needed. They are the most difficult part of your wardrobe to keep looking fresh.

➤ To keep clothes from sticking to your panty hose, apply a little Static Guard spray. Keep a can at home and at work.

➤ Avoid carrying bulky items such as your wallet or cell phone in jacket pockets, especially outside front pockets. This prevents pockets from sagging and the jacket from losing its clean lines. Carry these items in your handbag or tote.

➤ Remove everything from pockets before putting garments away. Items left in the pockets of jackets or pants cause the garments to stretch.

- Hang clothes so they fall *naturally*. This doesn't mean you have to sacrifice closet space by hanging each item inches apart. It means you should avoid cramming your clothes together. Cramming will leave hanger marks and indentations that may not come out.
- Use hangers that are the appropriate size for the garment. For example, don't use a small hanger on a large jacket. The hanger should go as near to the end of the shoulder as possible to help maintain the garment's shape.

TIP: *Have a Resource Bank*

Remember, Visual Therapy is all about being proactive, not reactive. Maintain a bank of resources you can rely on in case of emergencies or for when you may need something done quickly. Your "resource bank" should include: a shoe repairer; a dry cleaner for regular cleaning; a specialty dry cleaner whose expertise is difficult repairs and hard-to-remove stains; a good tailor (the right fit can make or break an outfit, and realistically, most clothing will need some alteration, even if minor, to fit properly); and a personal shopper or the salespeople at different stores with whom you have established a relationship as a good customer (if you are loyal to them, they will go the extra mile for you). Keep your resource bank, including addresses, phone numbers, and any other useful contact information, in a small address book or on file in your computer for quick access.

Dos and Don'ts

Nothing looks worse than a shirt with its buttons hanging by a thread! Sew them on securely, clip threads, and check hems regularly to make sure they are not loose and falling. Also, ironing can create a shine on fabric. To prevent this, do a soft-touch pressing of the garment by placing a thin cloth between it and the iron. This will protect the clothing from getting shiny as well as from any dirt or soil that may be on the iron. You can request your dry cleaner to do a soft-touch press on your garments, too.

Cleaning Knits

➤ Fold garments that go on shelves or in drawers with tissue paper to help maintain their shape and to avoid stretching and wrinkles when stored. Place the heaviest items always on the bottom.

➤ After wearing and before putting them away, air sweaters and other garments overnight to help maintain their freshness.

➤ Shave sweaters when they begin to pill to keep them from looking tired. If you wait until the sweater is too far gone before shaving it, it will be a lost cause. To shave sweaters correctly, place them on a hard, flat surface. Move the shaver over the sweater slowly, pressing down *lightly*. If you press too hard you risk putting a hole in it.

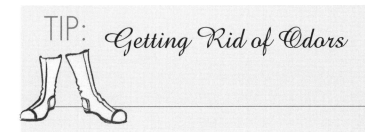

TIP: *Getting Rid of Odors*

If you are exposed to cigarette smoke, food, or any other odors that get into your clothes, use Febreze, a safe, instant spray refresher that eliminates unpleasant odors from clothing (as well as furniture). After you spray clothes, hang them on a hook or shower rod to air them out. Don't worry, Febreze won't stain or change the color.

Cleaning Shoes

➤ Keep shoes polished and stored on shoetrees to prevent them from aging quickly. Even the most expensive pair of shoes will age fast if not properly cared for.

➤ Immediately put rubber sole protectors on each new pair of shoes you buy to keep the sole from wearing out.

➤ Give shoes a thorough polish on a regular basis. For emergencies, or when traveling, carry an "instant shoeshine kit" (available at a cobbler or a better drugstore) with you. It looks like a small sponge and has the polishing agent already applied so you can do a quick shine anytime, anywhere.

Dos and Don'ts

Don't disobey the care instructions on garments. If the instructions say, "Dry-clean only," then dry-clean it only. However, if you are careful, you can hand-wash some "dry-clean only" knits in cold water with Woolite. This product prevents fading or bleeding colors. Also, don't dry garments on hangers. As they dry, the shape of the hanger remains in them. Consider buying a drying rack (it looks like a little mesh table that folds up); this rack allows garments to lay flat and dry thoroughly by being exposed to air on both sides.

Cleaning Lingerie

- For the best care, hand-wash rather than machine-wash your intimate apparel. Your lingerie will clean better, feel better on you, and last longer than if machine-washed. Inspect your lingerie (and all other garments, as well) before putting them away in closets or drawers.

Dos and Don'ts

Don't overclean. It is not necessary to clean a pant, jacket, or dress after *every* wearing. Dry cleaners can damage your clothing if overused because dry-cleaning fluid breaks down fiber. Overcleaning will also fade your blacks. If an item is wrinkled it can be steamed or pressed. Only dry-clean when absolutely necessary, especially jackets.

Pack Smart — The Visual Therapy Way

Packing smart is crucial to maintaining your personal style while traveling for business or pleasure. Packing is an extension of everything you have learned in Visual Therapy—that less is more, and that it is important to love what you wear (and take with you).

Never take things straight from your closet and put them in your suitcase. This will result in overpacking. You want to simplify and streamline your wardrobe when traveling so that you are not weighed down by carrying more clothes than you will wear. Editing your travel wardrobe is crucial. Put together more looks with fewer pieces, and you will have packed smart. Remember pieces that multitask.

Editing Your Travel Wardrobe

A great way to select what to take with you and avoid overpacking is to draw up a list of what you will need for each day's events in your travel schedule. This list will assist you in making your packing choices and help keep you organized while on the road.

The first thing to consider is how many days you will be away. This will tell you how many "day looks" versus "evening looks" you'll need. Next, lay out what you think you need on your bed and select outfits that will make the transition easily from day to evening with a simple change of accessories. A business look could be a dress with a matching jacket and a pair of pumps. For evening, lose the jacket, add a wrap, exchange the pumps for something strappy, swap your day bag for a clutch, and you are off and running.

The method of creating many different combos from a handful of pieces and accessories (multitasking from Steps #3 and #4 to keep your closet under control) is equally useful here to keep the weight of your luggage under control.

Following are some guidelines for editing your travel wardrobe and creating your travel wardrobe list (some of our clients take the photos of looks with them):

➤ Select a core capsule wardrobe.
➤ Choose tops, shoes, and bags that complement the core capsule pieces.
➤ Use accessories, scarves, or wraps for color and to change looks while on the road.
➤ Be sure everything you take can be worn with more than one outfit.

- As solids are more versatile than patterns while traveling, take comfortable black separates that are interchangeable for all occasions. To break things up add denim, underpinnings, or accessories for color.
- Wear your heaviest shoes, clothes, and outerwear on the plane to allow more room in your luggage. Pack other shoes you will be taking in shoe bags.
- Always carry jewelry, watches, medicine, a toothbrush, and travel documents on your person, not packed away, in case luggage is misplaced or lost.

TIP: *Vacation Traveling*

If you plan to travel to a warm (or beach) climate, instead of running out and purchasing new beachwear, check the "resort" section in your closet; you may well find the appropriate pieces there. Make a list of which items might be missing, and fill in these gaps when you arrive at your destination.

Just Wondering . . .

What if I am traveling to another city or part of the country to relocate? Relocating can sometimes be like traveling to another planet. Think about it: New York and Los Angeles, Chicago and Las Vegas, Miami and Seattle. How different can places be from each other? If you move from New York to Los Angeles and wear exactly the same look, you will appear out of place—and feel that way. You will want to capture the vibe and lifestyle of the place you are moving to and at first you may be tempted to dump everything and start over. Do not betray your declared style. If changes or modifications are necessary (to address climate issues, for example), figure out which items in your wardrobe work and which don't, and begin your new list of wants and needs by repeating Steps #2 through #4 of the Visual Therapy process as soon as you arrive in your new home.

Packing Your Suitcase

Your luggage should be as efficient as a filing cabinet, as presentable as your core wardrobe, and practical enough to transport your carefully chosen looks to and from your destination. A folding garment bag with wheels is helpful. You can wheel your hanging pieces neatly hung and folded with your second matching bag on top.

Here are some packing guidelines to follow:

➤ Place moisturizers and creams in Ziploc bags to avoid leakage.
➤ Belts should run along the perimeter of the inside of your suitcase to protect them.

- Pack bulky or heavy items, such as your shoes and toiletry kit, to the sides of your suitcase to prevent them from shifting, crushing, or weighing on clothes.
- Between each layer of clothing you pack, add tissue paper to prevent items from sliding and becoming excessively wrinkled.
- Fold pants at the crease or seam and lay across the suitcase with the bottom of the legs hanging over while you add a layer of tissue paper and place knits on top of open pants.
- Hanging garments (shirts and other pieces) should be placed individually into plastic bags—the kind they come in from the dry cleaner. Accumulate bags for just this purpose, or ask your dry cleaner for extra ones.
- Use a large Ziploc bag—or plastic baggie—to store worn undergarments until your return.

Keep Things in Perspective

Now that you have completed the five-step Visual Therapy process and always look your best and feel fabulous, remember this: Life is not only about fashion image and style. More important, it's about good health, friends, family, loved ones, pets, and finding meaning in our lives.

Balance and beauty, on the inside and on the outside, are things to strive for every day, in everything we do, in how we feel about ourselves and how we present ourselves to the world. It is our goal on this planet to live our best lives. Reconciling our image and our identity is one way to do that.

Visual Therapy's Three Golden Rules for Great Style

1. **You are the foundation.** It goes without saying that before choosing to wear any outfit, it is important to be healthy, clean, and well groomed. Every aspect of your grooming, from your hair to your nails to the fragrance you wear, are part of the mix. A fresh face and bright smile is the basis for every great look; without them, no outfit, no matter how tailored or expensive, will transform you.

2. **Less is truly more.** Sometimes, keeping it tastefully simple will draw more attention to you instead of all your accessories.

3. **A great fit says it all.** Clothes should never be too tight or too baggy. Spend a little extra to tailor your clothes if needed. A good tailor, lighting, and a three-way mirror will help you see what is appropriate.

In Case You Were Wondering . . .

(COMMONLY ASKED QUESTIONS FROM CLIENTS)

Q: **What do I wear to a daytime wedding?**
A: A dress, not pants or separates. A wedding is a time to be feminine and ladylike. It can be tastefully sexy but not va-va-voom.

Q: What is festive attire?

A: Something happy, fun—perhaps with some form of embellishment—colorful, and offbeat, but not super-sexy. Something you are able to celebrate and dance in.

Q: What is considered "black tie"?

A: A full-length evening gown and your most formal jewelry. Shoes should be silk, satin, or metallic. This is a good time to be dramatic, tastefully sexy, and regal.

Q: What is considered cocktail attire?

A: Basically, it is safe to keep everything to the knee, be it a simple dress or an embellished skirt with a sexy camisole. Such things definitely read "cocktail." If you prefer to go more edgy or modern, a tuxedo or an evening pant with an interesting top (like a white organza blouse) is also appropriate. This is a good time to be more whimsical, fun, and expressive.

Q: What is a party dress?

A: Certainly not a simple black dress. This calls for a celebratory look—colorful, playful, and fun to dance in. A party dress can also be considered cocktail attire but is usually not as sparkly and formal.

Q: What is the rule of thumb on nude panty hose?

A: Most corporate environments require panty hose. Be sure to choose a neutral style that is most natural to your leg. (You never want the "grandma-bologna-hose" look!) In other settings, the best look for legs is simply smooth, shiny skin, without panty hose. This always adds a more youthful, fresh look.

Q: When do I know my look is stale or dated?

A: Five years is a good indicator (and that is being generous). Always remember, your style file should be a frame of reference. If what you have in your closet is completely different than what you have in your file, you need to go shopping!

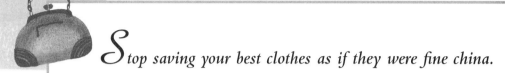

*S**top saving your best clothes as if they were fine china.***

Q: What do I do with accessories?

A: Wear them! And if you don't, get rid of them. As with your wardrobe, you must continuously edit, update, and upgrade your jewelry and other accessories. Apply the three Qs to your jewelry, belts, bags, scarves, and hats. Beware of the big wad of earrings or necklaces that become attached to each other. Compartmentalize your jewelry drawer or box. Your belts are either to hold up a pair of pants, complete a look, or emphasize a waistline—so be sure they fulfill one of these tasks (and fall within your defined style). An accessories edit is a good time to reaffirm your commitment to quality over quantity. Don't hang on to a belt because it came with an ensemble you no longer even own. Some women enjoy purchasing bags, scarves, and shoes because they never have to relate these things to their size, or simply because they collect them. You need to recognize *why* you buy and keep these things.

Q: What do I wear when I am the guest of honor or host?

A: This is your time to shine, to stand out in the crowd. You have free rein to dress as expressively as you please. This is one of the few occasions when it is acceptable to be slightly overdressed.

About the Authors

Jesse Garza is one of the country's most successful style gurus. His clients—professional and influential women from around the country—turn to him for direction and focus in creating their optimal style.

Garza began his career at Chicago's premier high-end boutique, Ultimo—an education he describes as "the Harvard School for Fashion." Eight years later, he became Ultimo's creative director and Chicago's leading arbiter of style.

In 1995, Garza left Chicago for New York City and cofounded Visual Therapy with Joe Lupo. Dubbed the "style SWAT team" by fashion editors, Garza and Lupo are behind some of the most popular images across the fashion landscape. Building on a collection of loyal clients, Garza now travels around the country teaching his clients the Visual Therapy way.

Garza has been quoted as a style expert in numerous publications, including *O, The Oprah Magazine*; *Harper's Bazaar*; *New York Magazine*; and *InStyle*.

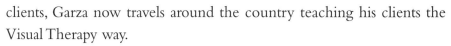

Joe Lupo is sought by public figures, media, and some of the largest luxury brands for help in creating a more authentic public image. He has appeared on VH1, the Fine Living Network's *The MANual* and *World Class with Frederique*, and is often quoted in major fashion and lifestyle publications for his expert advice on fashion and style. He is also a contributing writer for *V Man* magazine and *Bentley* magazine.

In 1995, Lupo cofounded Visual Therapy with Jesse Garza. Capitalizing on his background in corporate culture, Lupo manages Visual Therapy's corporate consulting services, which range from public relations to styling to event production, and he also works with the company's male private clients. Visual Therapy's list of corporate clients have included: Audi, Volkswagen, Bentley Motors, Maggie Norris, Oxxford Clothes, Julie Baker Designs, J. Mendel, and Legend Mink.

In 1998, Visual Therapy began consulting on *The Oprah Winfrey Show*, becoming responsible for the looks featured on some of the show's highly rated makeover and seasonal fashion shows.